FELICIA CARTRIGHT

AND THE CASE OF THE
ANTIQUE BOOKMARK

Felicia   Joan

FELICIA CARTRIGHT

AND THE CASE OF THE
ANTIQUE BOOKMARK

BERNARD PALMER

Aneko Press *Youth*

www.anekopress.com

Aneko Press, Life Sentence Publishing, and our logos are trademarks of
Life Sentence Publishing, Inc.
203 E. Birch Street
P.O. Box 652
Abbotsford, WI 54405

JUVENILE FICTION / Religious / Christian / Action & Adventure

Paperback ISBN: 979-8-88936-304-0

eBook ISBN: 979-8-88936-305-7

10 9 8 7 6 5 4 3 2 1

Available where books are sold

CONTENTS

CHAPTER 1

AN ACCUSATION

Winifred Stromer, dark eyes flashing and twin spots of anger burning hot and red in her cheeks, opened the cabin door and approached Felicia Cartright and Joan Bailey. Felicia looked up, smiling.

"Good morning, Winnie."

For a moment, the girl before them did not speak. Her lips parted slightly, and her small hands clenched until the knuckles showed white. She was tall for her fourteen years and slight of build; an attractive girl despite the pout that seemed to rest perpetually on her mouth.

"Is there something we can do for you?" Felicia asked.

That seemed to loosen her tongue. "I–I've just got to talk with you, Miss Cartright!" she blurted.

Joan got to her feet, tossed her large beach towel over her shoulders, and flashed a quick smile at the young camper. "You can talk to Felicia alone now," she said. "I've got a swimming class." She went out the door. "I'll see you at lunch, Felicia."

Winnie Stromer watched Joan leave. "She–she didn't have to go," she managed uncertainly, "W-W-What I've got to talk to you about isn't any secret."

Felicia smiled reassuringly. This was something of a milestone – the first girl who had come in for guidance since she and Joan began to counsel at Camp in the Pines ten days before. "Won't you sit down?"

Winnie did not move. "You're going to have to do something about that Mary Jane!"

The smile left Felicia's face and her eyes grew serious. "What do you mean?"

Now that she had started to talk, the words gushed out vehemently. "She stole five dollars from me. That's what she did! She took it from my purse!"

Felicia fought to keep from revealing her shock at Winnie's charge. "That's a serious accusation," she said, managing to keep her voice even. "Are you sure you didn't spend the money and forget about it? That happens to me sometimes."

"I just broke a ten-dollar bill yesterday," Winnie informed her, "and I only spent two dollars."

"Perhaps you lost the five-dollar bill."

She shook her head. "I didn't lose it, and I didn't spend it," she said belligerently. "It was in my purse when I looked this morning before I went to breakfast. I went to get it just now, and it was gone! Mary Jane stole it!"

There was a short silence.

"And what makes you think that Mary Jane is the one who took your money?" Felicia persisted. "You must have some reason."

Winnie's young mouth tightened angrily. "You know how she's always hanging around the cabin, even when we're supposed to be having archery, canoeing, or handcraft?" the Stromer girl went on.

Felicia nodded. It was true that either she or Joan had to go to the cabin and get Mary Jane Forbes to come and take part in the various camp activities once or twice a day, but Felicia had attributed that to her extreme shyness. Her shyness and the way the rest of the girls ignored her and left her out of things.

"Well, she was the only one left in the cabin when I went to breakfast this morning. And when she came into the dining hall, I said something to her, but she blushed and–and couldn't even look at me. I know now that she felt guilty because she had taken my money."

Felicia Cartright got to her feet slowly, praying for wisdom and guidance, and put her arm around Winnie's young shoulder. "I'm so glad you came to me about this," she said, "instead of talking to all the girls in camp about Mary Jane."

"You'll see about it, won't you?" Winnie's eyes sought hers.

"I'll look into it," Felicia promised, "but I'm going to ask you to do something for me."

They walked to the cabin door together.

"Please don't say anything to any of the other girls

about this, Winnie – especially that you suspect Mary Jane. She may have had a perfectly logical reason for being in the cabin when you left this morning, and there's a very good chance that she doesn't know anything about your money."

Winnie shrank away from Felicia and looked up at her. "Are you going to stick up for her?" she demanded.

"I just want to be sure that we're right before we say anything to anyone," Felicia answered. "We may be doing Mary Jane a terrible injustice."

"I won't say anything to anyone about it," Winnie agreed reluctantly, "but I know she's the one who did it. She has to be!"

Felicia tightened her grip on the girl's shoulder momentarily. "Have you prayed for her?" she asked.

Winnie Stromer stared at her questioningly, then turned and walked away. Felicia watched until the girl went into the camp canteen, disappearing from view. Then she turned and went back to the table where she had been studying for the next day's Bible lesson. But somehow, she could not get her mind on the lesson. Questions whirled unanswered in her mind.

What of Mary Jane? Had she actually stolen the money? She was a quiet, unhappy girl. That much was true. Somewhere Felicia had heard that girls of that sort often did resort to disobedience and theft.

Resolutely, Felicia got to her feet and, picking up her Bible and study books, started down the path to the double cabin where she and Joan were counselors, each with six girls.

CHAPTER 2

CAMP IN THE PINES

Felicia Cartright and Joan Bailey had not planned on working at Camp in the Pines that summer. In fact, they had never heard of the Maine Bible camp until Dr. Warren Markington and his wife sought them out at Wellington early in May.

"Our camp is different than most Bible camps," he began. "We take youngsters in for the entire summer and give them intensive Bible training along with a varied camping program."

Felicia looked at Joan and back at their callers quizzically.

"We thought we had all of our counselors six months ago," Mrs. Markington explained, "but we received a message last week that two of the girls are going to be unable to come."

"So," the man said, "I contacted your pastor, and he highly recommended you girls."

He breathed deeply. "It isn't a job that will pay you well," he went on, "and I don't have to tell you that it's hard work with little time off. But there's something rewarding about working with young people that has kept us at it for twenty-eight years."

"Camping provides a wonderful opportunity to deal with the girls spiritually," Mrs. Markington said. "I can speak from personal experience."

"I don't know what to tell you at the moment," Felicia said, trying to read Joan's reaction in her dark, oval face. "Could we let you know later?"

"You could give us an answer in a couple of days, couldn't you?"

"Oh, yes," Joan said quickly.

"Why don't you talk it over and let us know as soon as you do decide?" Dr. Markington suggested.

The kindly, gray-haired couple had just left the dorm when Felicia turned to Joan. "Well, what do you think?" she asked.

Joan tossed her dark hair and wrinkled her little button nose. "I was all set to have a leisurely summer at home," she said, "sleeping until noon and going to a different party every night."

She got to her feet. "I don't suppose there's a boy within a hundred miles of the place."

Felicia laughed. "Oh, yes," she said, "there's Camp in the Pines for girls and Camp in the Cedars for boys – right next to it."

"Sure," Joan retorted disdainfully, "there'll be lots of little boys. A great help that'll be to us."

"Little boys will have to have big boys for counselors," Felicia reminded her. "Not that we'd have time to spend with them if they did ask us. We'll be busy with our campers."

"That's the trouble with you," Joan countered. "You're a pessimist." The laughter died in her eyes. "Seriously though, Felicia, it sounds like a wonderful way to spend the summer."

"That's the way it seems to me."

Before Dr. Markington and his wife had time to leave the campus, the girls had decided to spend the summer counseling at Camp in the Pines.

Felicia and Joan had ten days to rest between the close of school and the preseason training period for counselors.

"I can't see the idea of coming here for a whole week of training," Joan said as she wheeled her bright red convertible off the main highway to the narrow, twisting trail that led to the camp. "We've done counseling before."

"Dr. Markington told us that they expect a great deal from their counselors in the way of guidance and helping the girls with personal and spiritual problems," Felicia said. "I'm glad for the chance to learn."

"So am I, really," Joan confessed, "but you know lazy old me. I don't like to do any more than I have to do. I keep thinking of all those mornings we're going to have to get up early."

The time they spent in the preseason training period was more enjoyable than they had hoped. The rest of the counselors were about their age, and they had great times on picnics, hikes, and canoe trips through the wilderness area. And through it all, Dr. and Mrs. Markington taught them how to conduct the informal Bible studies each counselor would have with the girls of her cabin and how to recognize personality problems and to deal with them.

Time passed quickly, and it wasn't long until the day came for the campers to arrive. Felicia and Joan had already been assigned a double cabin and were to have six girls each. They went out with the other counselors to meet the bus.

Mary Jane Forbes was the first to get off. Felicia Cartright would never forget that

She stepped down hesitantly, a battered suitcase in her hand. About Winifred Stromer's age, Felicia learned later, she was shorter than the other girls. She was neat and clean, and her sandy hair was attractively done; but her dress gave the appearance of separating at the seams as though it had been worn by someone who was too big for it. Her accessories were cute, but obviously the gift of a year or two before by someone who had grown tired of them.

Mary Jane stood to one side looking about uncomfortably at the campers who were all laughing and talking at once. Felicia watched her for a minute or two.

A faint smile came to her lips now and again, and it was plain that she wanted to join the others but did not quite know how. So instead, she shifted the suitcase from one hand to the other and watched while her companions streamed, jabbering excitedly, from the bus.

Felicia's eye caught her almost immediately as the other girls surged around her.

"Cindy's going to be my bunk mate," someone sang out in a shrill voice. "Cindy Prescott and I are together."

"And Donna Cramer and I are together," another girl called.

Mrs. Markington blew her whistle to quiet them. "Welcome to Camp in the Pines!" she exclaimed. "We're all going to have a good time here this summer."

She paused until they were completely quiet. "Get your gear and go down to the administration building as quickly as possible," she said. "We want to get you registered and into your cabins before lunch."

The girls surged toward the bus driver who was busy unloading suitcases and duffel bags.

Felicia went over to the slight, sandy-haired girl who was still standing alone. "Hello," she said.

The girl looked up, smiling weakly.

"My name is Miss Cartright," Felicia said easily. "How would you like to be in my cabin?"

There was a brief hesitation.

"I–I think I'd like that if you have room."

9

"We'll see the registrar," Felicia told her, "and make sure there's room."

She put her arm around Mary Jane's shoulder. "Is this all of your luggage?"

She nodded.

Felicia took her down to the administration building, talked with the girl who was doing the registering, and got Mary Jane assigned to her cabin. Then they went over to the cabin and Felicia helped her hang up her clothes and make her bed.

Mary Jane smiled a little now and then, and when she did, her entire being seemed to shine.

"Who's the prodigy?" Joan asked softly sometime later when the other girls came jostling into the double cabin.

"Mary Jane Forbes," Felicia whispered. "And I can't figure her out. She's such a shy, retiring little thing."

Joan nodded. "Leave it to you," she whispered. "You'd find someone to mother."

Felicia wrinkled her nose at her.

During the next two or three days, Felicia Cartright tried to get next to Mary Jane and make friends with her. The younger girl responded in a pathetic, half-hearted way, but her reserve seemed to hold her back.

And now this!

A shudder danced up Felicia's spine. Mary Jane couldn't be the one who had stolen Winnie Stromer's money! She just couldn't!

A desperate prayer arose!

CHAPTER 3

FELICIA IS TROUBLED

Felicia went down to her cabin hoping that Mary Jane Forbes would be there so she could talk with her, but she was not. There was no one in the big sleeping cabin. For a moment or two, she looked around uneasily. Then she walked over to Mary Jane's bed and looked down at her tattered suitcase.

It was a temptation to open it and look inside. The girls were all down swimming and would be for another twenty minutes or so. She could look and satisfy herself whether the girl had a five-dollar bill or not.

But no, she could not do that unless Mary Jane were there and gave her permission. And besides, one five-dollar bill was very much the same as another. Even if she did have one, it would prove nothing one way or the other.

Felicia went over and sat down. A dull headache

nagged at her senses, and a bone-deep weariness seemed to have taken hold of her suddenly.

What could she do to find out who stole Winnie's money? How could she help Mary Jane Forbes?

She was still sitting there when Joan came in on the heels of a tribe of wet, excited girls.

"That's a workout!" Joan exclaimed, sagging into a chair. "I feel as though I've just run twenty miles."

Felicia's eyes sought hers.

"Hurry up and get dressed," she said softly. "I'd like to talk to you."

Joan saw her concern. "Is it about Winnie?" she asked.

"Yes and no."

Felicia and Joan had to stay in the cabin until the girls changed and were on their way to the dining room for lunch, so it was half an hour or more before they could be alone together.

"Now what is it?" Joan asked, joining her friend on the steps. "You act upset."

"I am a little," Felicia answered. "In fact, I'm more than a little upset. I'm terribly concerned."

Hurriedly, she told Joan of Winnie Stromer's accusation against Mary Jane.

"I know this sort of thing happens once in a while, even at Christian camps," she concluded, "but a girl like Mary Jane! I tried not to let Winnie know I was shocked, but I couldn't have been more surprised if she had accused you or me."

"I'll have to agree," Joan answered, "it certainly doesn't sound much like Mary Jane."

"She just isn't that kind of a girl," Felicia said. "I'd almost stake my life on it." She paused and leaned against a huge, smooth-barked beech tree.

"What are you going to do?" Joan asked.

"That's what I don't know. I promised Winnie I'd look into it. I'll have to do something."

"That might not be so easy."

"That's what worries me."

The dining bell rang, and the few late stragglers broke into a run.

Felicia and Joan started down the path once more. "You could call Mary Jane in and talk with her," Joan said.

"That's what I had in mind when I came down to the cabin after Winnie talked with me. Now I'm glad she wasn't there. I don't think talking to her would accomplish anything, and it might do a lot of harm. Mary Jane is so sensitive."

Felicia went to see Mrs. Markington after lunch and told her what had happened. The camp director folded her pudgy hands on her desk, and for a time, the look in her eyes grew far away.

"That is unfortunate," she said. "For the sake of the girl who's doing the stealing, we must find out who she is so we can stop her before it's too late."

Felicia nodded. "I thought at first that I would call her in and talk with her as kindly as I knew how, but the more I think of it, the more afraid I am that it wouldn't be the thing. As I told Joan, Mary Jane is so sensitive."

"Mary Jane is sensitive," Mrs. Markington agreed, "and very poor."

"I gathered as much when I saw her suitcase and her clothes," Felicia hesitated. "I couldn't help wondering how she was able to come here for the summer. I know that it's quite expensive."

"One of the wealthier members of the church she attends paid her way. Her parents are so proud they were reluctant to let her come on that basis at first until the pastor was able to convince them it was best for Mary Jane."

Mrs. Markington continued to tell Felicia what she knew of the Forbes girl's background. When she finished, the young counselor leaned forward.

"What do you think I should do?" she asked.

"I think you're following a wise course," she told her, smiling her approval. "In anything like this, it is always wisest to wait until you are sure of your ground before you act. I shall leave the matter entirely in your hands."

Felicia got to her feet. "Thank you, Mrs. Markington."

"We'll be praying for you."

That evening after the campfire service, Winifred Stromer sought out Felicia. "Did you talk to Mary Jane?" she asked.

She shook her head. "I went to Mrs. Markington," she answered, "and we decided that we are going to wait until we uncover more evidence that points to Mary Jane or someone else before we do anything."

Looking down at the dark-haired camper, Felicia read the disappointment in Winnie's eyes, but she said nothing.

During the next few days, Felicia Cartright and Joan Bailey tried to keep a close watch on the girls in their cabin and to find out more about them and what they did. They took special care, too, to be sure the girls kept their belongings put away so that no one would be tempted to take anything more.

"We want each of you to turn your money in to Joan or to me," Felicia told them. "We'll give you receipts for it and let you have it whenever you want it."

Cindy Prescott looked up questioningly. "What's this all about?" she asked. "Has somebody been stealing something?"

"We want to be sure that it doesn't happen," Joan answered.

Felicia got quickly to her feet. "You're dismissed now, but remember what I told you. Right after our rest period this afternoon, you can bring your money to us."

Mary Jane hung back until after the others were gone. "M-Miss Cartright," she began uncertainly, "I–I don't have any money."

Felicia looked at her questioningly. "Not even for stamps and a little candy or pop?"

She shook her head. "Dad got me some postcards before I came, and he said that he–he'd try to send me some money later." Her voice faltered and her face flushed scarlet at the confession, "but he's been sick and hasn't been working regularly. My parents need everything he can make w-w-without sending money for me to spend."

Felicia told Joan about it later. "You know," she said, "it isn't even circumstantial evidence, but that certainly would give Mary Jane a motive for taking money. Imagine what it must be like to see all the other kids buying things at the canteen and never being able to buy anything yourself."

"I'm going to see that she gets a little money to spend," Joan said, "if I have to hire her to work for me here in the cabin."

The next few days were a duplication of the others. Mary Jane stayed on the fringe of activity, passive and uncommunicative. Both Felicia and Joan tried, without success, to draw her into things.

"Tomorrow night is skit night," Felicia confided to her one noon. "I'd like to have you head our cabin group and work out a skit for us to give."

Mary Jane looked up. Interest flickered in her eyes for a moment or two before dying away. "I–I don't think I could."

"Of course, you can," Felicia assured her. "I'll help you if you'd like. I'm sure you have a lot of good ideas."

The uncertainty came back. "No, thank you, Miss Cartright," she stammered, "I–I don't think I can."

The following morning the campers were all supposed to be swimming when Felicia surprised Mary Jane in their cabin. She was standing beside Felicia's bed, looking at something intently.

Ice formed in the young counselor's veins. "Why Mary Jane!" she exclaimed, "what are you doing here?"

The girl turned, her face ashen. "I–I was just looking at this," she said lamely. She had Felicia's Bible in one hand and the antique bookmark that had been her great-grandmother's in the other.

Felicia came over to her.

"It–it's beautiful," Mary Jane said. "It's the most beautiful bookmark I've ever seen in my whole life."

Felicia's voice softened. "I feel the same way about it," she said. "It's one of the most treasured things I have."

She took the bookmark and looked at it again. It was embroidered of gold and silver thread with a small cross of rubies at the top and a Bible reference worked into the design. Its very old age was apparent at a glance.

"Where did you get it, Miss Cartright?" Mary Jane asked.

Felicia smiled. "It's time you were in swimming, young lady, and the story of the bookmark is a long one. I'll tell you what I'll do. After devotions tonight, I'll tell you and the other girls all about it."

"Oh, thank you." She flashed a thin smile and went off toward the beach where the others had been swimming for ten minutes or more.

Felicia Cartright watched her uneasily. It was strange that she would be the only one in the cabin when Winnie's five-dollar bill was stolen and that she would be in the cabin alone now. It was very strange indeed.

Felicia took her Bible and put it away thoughtfully.

CHAPTER 4

A SHINING TESTIMONY

Winnie Stromer and the other girls in Oriole Cabin took part in the skit at the campfire that night. All, that is, except Mary Jane Forbes. She sat on the sidelines, watching wistfully. Felicia's heart ached for her.

As usual, Joan Bailey's Ravens won first prize with an original little skit that had them all rolling with laughter. On the way back to the cabin when it was over, the girls were in a happy mood.

"Oh, Miss Cartright," Mary Jane said, coming up beside Felicia shyly and taking her by the hand, "wasn't that the funniest thing you ever saw?"

A smile glinted in Felicia's eyes. "It was funny," she agreed.

They walked on for a few yards in silence.

"Don't Christians have more fun than anybody?" Mary Jane said.

Felicia stopped and let the other girls go on ahead of them. "That's something I've been wanting to talk with you about, Mary Jane," she began quietly. "Are you a Christian? Do you know the Lord as your Savior?"

Mary Jane's soft blue eyes looked up to hers. "Oh, yes," she said, "I've been a Christian for several years. We were having special meetings at the church when I was in the third or fourth grade, and I trusted Christ as my Savior."

"I'm so glad to know that." Felicia put her arm around the girl's shoulder and squeezed her affectionately. "Living for Christ is the most important thing in all the world."

In the double cabin, the Orioles and Ravens were going to have devotions together. Joan Bailey had them seated and quiet before Felicia entered with Mary Jane. She opened the time with prayer and turned it over to her friend and fellow counselor.

"We've had a lot of fun tonight," Felicia began, "As Mary Jane said tonight, 'Don't Christians have more fun than anybody?'"

Two or three girls nodded solemnly, but Winnie Stromer snorted her disgust.

Felicia opened her Bible to the third chapter of John, read it thoughtfully, and explained the way of salvation step by step.

"The first thing anyone must do," she said, "is to recognize that he is a sinner and needs a Savior. Can any of you give a Bible verse that tells us that?"

There was a moment's hesitation; then Mary Jane's thin arm went up. "Romans 6:23," she said, "*The wages of sin is death; but the gift of God is eternal life through Jesus Christ our Lord.*"

"That's fine, Mary Jane," Felicia said.

The girl's face paled as the counselor called attention to her, and she looked away.

"Now," the leader went on, "can anybody give us another verse that would help a person to accept Christ?"

There was another long hesitation before Mary Jane's hand went up again. "Romans 10:9," she said, her voice faltering. "says that if you confess with your mouth the Lord Jesus and believe in your heart that God has raised Him from the dead, you will be saved. For with the heart man believes unto righteousness; and with the mouth confession is made unto salvation." She swallowed hard. "That–that was Romans 10:9 and 10," she blurted.

"I am wondering," Felicia said, looking from one girl to another deliberately, "have you accepted Christ as your Savior? It is something that each of you must do – a decision you must make personally."

She did not ask for an answer, but several girls nodded, and two gave a brief testimony. At last, her gaze came to rest on Winnie. The tall, dark-haired girl colored first, then her face went white. Her lips parted slightly before she looked away.

"If any of you would like to talk with Joan or

me either this evening or at any other time," she concluded, "we'd be so happy to go over the way of salvation with you."

After prayer, the girls went thoughtfully to bed, and Joan and Felicia went out into the still night air to sit on the porch for a moment or two.

"Well," Joan said, keeping her voice down, "we learned a number of things tonight. Mary Jane may be quiet and slow to enter into the day's activities, but she certainly puts the rest of them to shame when it comes to knowing the Scriptures."

"I rather thought that she was a Christian before," Felicia said, "but there's no doubt at all in my mind now that she is a Christian."

"Nor mine."

There was a short silence. They looked up at the stars that seemed to be suspended just beyond the treetops. From the nearby lake came the discordant yet vaguely interesting croaking of a galaxy of frogs.

"What about Winnie?" Joan asked.

"She was under conviction tonight," Felicia answered. "I'm sure of it. I happened to be watching her when Mary Jane was quoting those passages of Scripture. Every word seemed to hit her hard."

"I suppose she was thinking about that money she says Mary Jane stole from her," the Bailey girl said.

Felicia straightened. "You know," she said, "I can't believe that Mary Jane would steal anything; but this morning when she was supposed to be swimming, I found her in the cabin looking at the bookmark that used to belong to my great-grandmother."

"That would be something," Joan said, "if the girl with the best sounding testimony in either of our groups would turn out to be a thief."

She sighed deeply. "I don't know of anything that would do more harm or make it harder to reach the others for Christ."

"No," Felicia said, "but I still can't believe that Mary Jane would take anything that doesn't belong to her. I can't help but have faith in her."

It was not until she got to bed that night that Felicia remembered that she hadn't told the girls the story of the bookmark as she had promised Mary Jane she would. That was one thing she would have to do the next day for sure.

She went to sleep to dream uneasily of Mary Jane, Winnie, and a whole list of things that had been stolen.

Felicia remembered the bookmark when she had her morning devotions alone in the cabin before the girls got up, but something happened after breakfast to cause her to forget it completely.

The girls trooped back to their cabin for the morning's Bible study, and Cindy Prescott squealed her dismay. "They're gone!" she cried. "They're gone!"

Everyone crowded around her, staring down at her suitcase.

"What's gone?" Felicia asked her, keeping her voice firm and emotionless.

"My two candy bars!" Cindy exclaimed. "I had them right here! Right in the front of my suitcase! But they're not here now! Someone must have stolen them!"

Felicia studied her carefully.

"And my swim goggles!" she moaned. "They're gone too!"

Joan Bailey heard her and came to the door between the two cabin rooms. Felicia's gaze sought hers helplessly.

CHAPTER 5

THE BOOKMARK MYSTERY

*S*ilence descended on the little group as the girls looked to their counselors.

"I think we had all better come in here and sit down," said Felicia.

She led them into the Raven's half of the big, two-roomed cabin and waited until they were seated in a tense semicircle on the floor.

"You girls know what has just happened," she said. "And I'm sure you realize how serious it is."

She let them think about her words. "First it was five dollars," she continued gravely. "Now it is a pair of goggles and two candy bars that have been stolen. Cindy said she paid over five dollars for the goggles just before she came up here; so this time things worth almost ten dollars were stolen. The next time it will probably be more unless the person who did it is discovered. That is the way such things go."

The girls were all eyeing Felicia somberly. They had not been so quiet – so tense – since they first came together.

"It is not the value of what is taken that makes it sin," she went on, grasping for words. "It is just as wrong to steal two candy bars and goggles as it is to steal a thousand dollars. The Bible tells us that the sin is in taking anything that belongs to someone else."

Winnie Stromer was the first to speak. "What are you going to do?" she asked, "Go through our suitcases and bedrolls?"

Felicia took a moment or two in answering. "No," she said finally, "I don't think we'll do anything as drastic as that – at least not for the present. I want to give the guilty person an opportunity to come to me and confess what she has done."

She waited for a long minute while the girls cringed uneasily. Then, turning in her Bible to the seventh chapter of Joshua, she read how Achan had stolen and about God's punishment for him.

"God isn't that harsh with us," she concluded. "The Bible tells us that God is faithful and just to forgive us our sins if we only confess them to Him and turn away from them."

She took a deep breath, and once more, her gaze went from one upturned face to another. "I'm going to talk now to the person or persons who stole Winnie's money and Cindy's candy and her goggles. We don't know who you are yet, although we will find out before long. But God knows. He knows everything you have done. He is talking to your heart right now, telling you that you should come to me and confess what you have done and make it right."

A bell rang signaling the end of the period, and she waited until it stopped. "Won't you come to me sometime today?" she asked, "and tell me that you are the one who took those things?"

When the girls were gone, Joan turned to Felicia. "I feel sick inside," she said. "To think this had to happen after last night – just when it seemed that we were beginning to get somewhere with them spiritually."

Felicia went over and sat down. "You know," she said, "I could just hear Winnie Stromer saying, 'I told you so,' while I was talking. I'm sure she still blames Mary Jane."

"She probably does. What I hope is that she doesn't start talking among the girls. I'm afraid the girls would all be glad to think that she is the guilty one."

"I'm afraid you're right." Their eyes met.

"I hope we get this straightened out before we go on the canoe trip. That's scheduled for the first of next week."

"So do I," Joan answered. "I'm hoping that the guilty person will come and talk to you sometime today, but for some reason I don't have much confidence in it. I'm afraid we'll have to find out for ourselves who's guilty."

Felicia's lips firmed. "I have been wondering if we ought to suggest to Mrs. Markington that we not take the canoe trip unless the guilty person is found."

Joan shook her head. "I'm afraid that might turn the girls terribly against whoever they might suspect. If they thought Mary Jane was guilty, they might give her a bad time whether she is or not."

"That's something I hadn't thought about."

That afternoon, Joan told the girls about the canoe trip they would be taking the following week and outlined the conditions each would have to meet in order to get to go.

"The canoe trips are really the highlight of the summer," she began, "and they are not dangerous if we all are able to take care of ourselves."

An arm went up. "What do you mean?" Winifred Stromer asked.

"We must have a certain proficiency in the skills that are required on a canoe trip. We must be able to handle a canoe, swim well, know the fundamentals of first aid, camping, cooking out of doors, and so on."

A groan escaped the lips of two or three girls in the back. "We might have known there would be a catch to it," one of them muttered.

"It's not going to be as bad as all of that," Felicia put in, smiling warmly. "Most of you can do those things well enough now to pass the requirements Mrs. Markington has set. And the rest of you have time enough to learn the things you don't know well between now and the time we will be going."

"There's a good reason for having requirements in a matter like this," Joan went on. "The Markingtons want to be very sure that there aren't any serious accidents and that none of you get into trouble and run the risk of getting hurt or drowned because you are permitted to do something before you are ready."

"There go my chances," Cindy Prescott said in an undertone. "I'll never be able to do it."

"Sure you will. I've been watching you swim, Cindy. I can tell you right now that you'll be able to pass your swimming test. And that's the most important."

Winifred Stromer squirmed uneasily. "It–it is?" she echoed. Felicia thought she detected concern in her voice.

"You can swim, can't you, Winnie?" she asked.

"Oh, yes," the girl retorted quickly. "I can swim, all right. I won't have any trouble with that test. Only–only it seemed strange to me that swimming would be so important."

She laughed. "But then, I guess if we upset a canoe, we'd have to be able to swim, wouldn't we?"

"We'll start work on the tests this afternoon," Joan concluded. "And I want you all to work as hard as you can because we don't want to have to leave anyone at home."

They got up and started down to the lake.

"I won't have to worry any," Winnie boasted. "I can do all of those things."

Felicia sought out Mary Jane. "The canoe trip sounds fun, doesn't it?" she asked.

The girl nodded wordlessly.

"Ever since we heard about it, Joan and I have been so anxious to go on it. I think we're even more excited about it than you girls are."

Near the water's edge, Felicia slowed her pace. "I've been watching you paddle, Mary Jane," she said, "and you handle a canoe so well. I think it would give the other girls confidence if you would pass the test first. Wouldn't you like to do that?"

She hesitated. "I–I don't know." The color came up into her cheeks.

"Sure you can." Felicia patted her on the shoulder reassuringly. She stepped out and blew her whistle.

"May I go first?" Winnie piped as soon as the girls were quiet. "May I go first?"

"I'm sorry," Felicia said, "but I've already asked Mary Jane to go first. You can be second."

Winnie's lip curled into an exaggerated pout.

Mary Jane stepped out uncertainly, launched her canoe, and got in. But once she was in the canoe, her uncertainty ceased. Ignoring the seat, she knelt in the bottom in the approved manner and demonstrated the basic strokes. She turned first in one direction and then the other, backed the canoe, and showed how to take it out of the water and carry it on a portage.

A gasp of admiration went up when she finished, and for an instant, she flushed with the pride of accomplishment.

"Now that," Joan said, "is as good as I have seen anyone handle a canoe. You must have had a lot of experience."

"I–I have," she stammered.

Winnie Stromer went next. She handled the canoe well enough but was sloppy and amateurish when compared with Mary Jane.

Four other girls passed their canoeing test that afternoon before the period was over.

"I wish I could handle a canoe like Mary Jane does," one of the girls said admiringly.

"So do I," Winnie retorted, her lips curling bitterly around the words, "but at least I don't take things that don't belong to me."

Felicia's gaze met Winnie's stonily, and she shook her head in disapproval. At least Mary Jane didn't hear her. She gave no sign. Or did she? Felicia could not be sure. You could never tell with a girl like Mary Jane.

Winifred's face paled. "I–I'm sorry," she said, her voice soft. "I didn't mean to say it. It just slipped out."

Joan and Felicia walked back to the cabin together.

"You finally got her to do something," Joan said, keeping her voice low so the kids who were streaming by would not hear.

"And did you see her?" Felicia exclaimed. "I was so proud of her! She handled her canoe like a veteran Maine guide."

They met Mrs. Markington on the path and stopped to talk for a minute or two.

"I didn't really think you would have anyone come and talk to you," the woman said, "but I was most curious about it. We've been praying about the whole matter – and especially for the girl who is doing the stealing. She's the one I feel the sorriest for in the whole affair. She's the one who stands to lose the most if she isn't found out and stopped."

It was fifteen minutes or so before Felicia and Joan left Mrs. Markington and went to their cabin.

Felicia entered the Oriole side. The big room was empty except for a blonde girl standing before the counselor's bed looking at something.

"Hello, Mary Jane," Felicia said, trying to hide her concern at finding her there.

Mary Jane turned, flushing scarlet. "E-e-excuse me, Miss Cartright," she stammered, "But I–I was just looking at your bookmark."

"That's quite all right," Felicia said. "I think it is beautiful myself."

And then she remembered. "It just occurred to me," she said apologetically, "that I promised to tell you about the bookmark and why it means so much to me, and I haven't done it yet, have I?"

Mary Jane shook her head.

"I'll tell you about it tonight for devotions," she promised, "and if I don't, you be sure and remind me."

But Felicia remembered herself.

That evening when the campfire service was over and the Orioles and Ravens were gathered together, she held up the bookmark for them to see.

"I don't know whether any of you girls besides Mary Jane has seen this bookmark or not."

They all leaned forward eagerly.

"I'll describe it to you first," she went on, "and tell you about it. Then I'll pass it around so you can each get a good look at it."

She turned the bookmark as she held it out for them to see. "First of all, I have to tell you that there is something of a mystery about this bookmark," she said. "It has been in our family for many, many years; and we have been told that it is almost a hundred and fifty years old, but we don't know where it came from or who made it. My grandmother says that all she knows about it is that her grandmother got it when she was just a girl."

"What's it made of?" Winifred Stromer wanted to know.

"I was just about to tell you, Winnie," Felicia continued. "It has been woven of gold and silver thread, and it has a small cross made of tiny rubies."

The girls gasped.

"The rubies are small," Felicia said, "and the use of gold and silver thread was not uncommon a hundred and fifty years ago among the very wealthy people; so that doesn't mean that this bookmark is worth a fabulous amount, although it is undoubtedly quite valuable."

"Did you ever find out how much it is worth?" Winnie broke in.

"No," Felicia smiled. "We haven't. Because, you see, this bookmark isn't for sale at any price. It means too much to me to even consider selling it."

"What do you mean?" one of the other girls wanted to know.

"This bookmark has a Scripture text woven into it," the young counselor said. "It is Romans 6:23. Can any of you tell us what it is and where you heard it?"

"Mary Jane quoted it," Cindy said, "It said something about the wages of sin being death, but I don't remember the rest of it."

"That's right. *The wages of sin is death; but the gift of God is eternal life through Jesus Christ our Lord.* My mother was one of those persons who believed that because her parents were Christians, she wouldn't have to be saved – that they had enough Christianity to get her to heaven too. Then on her sixteenth birthday, her mother gave her this bookmark. She looked up the verse and read it over until she memorized it."

Felicia's voice lowered gravely. "She said that verse kept hammering through her heart night after night until she realized that she was a sinner and needed the Savior. Not until then did she see that this was the only way she could possibly hope to be saved. She went to her mother – my grandmother – and made her decision to trust Christ."

Mary Jane Forbes was leaning forward, clinging

eagerly to every word. "Oh, Miss Cartright," she exclaimed when Felicia had finished, "that's a wonderful story!"

Felicia turned the meeting to Joan who patiently explained the way of salvation and the need for dedicating their lives to Christ after they have taken a stand for Him. When she finished, two girls came up to talk to them, and they had the privilege of leading them both to Christ.

It was the most wonderful time of devotions they had had since they came up to Camp in the Pines to serve as counselors. Felicia thought about it until she went to sleep that night, and the next morning when she awoke, she was reminded of it again.

The girls were still asleep when she dressed and reached for her Bible to have her own personal devotions. Usually she had put it away, but that night when the girls were finished looking at the bookmark, she had laid it on the little nightstand near her bed.

She held the Bible in her hand momentarily. The early morning sun was streaming through the window, flooding the big room with light. Everyone else was still asleep. In the room next to them even Joan, who was an early riser, had not yet stirred. Felicia could hear no sound except that of their slow, regular breathing. A prayer of thanksgiving for the girls who accepted Christ the night before went heavenward.

Then Felicia opened her Bible. For a long minute she stared at it. Her bookmark!

It was gone!

CHAPTER 6

THE SEARCH, A WARNING, AND A DISCOVERY

Felicia Cartright stared down at her open Bible. Her bookmark could not be gone! It had to be around somewhere! It just had to be!

She looked under the bed and on the floor around the nightstand, but it was not there.

She paused and tugged at the lobe of her ear thoughtfully. She didn't remember taking the bookmark from her Bible and putting it away by itself. That was something she never did. But she must have! That was the only explanation. Uneasily she went to her suitcase and opened it.

Hurriedly, Felicia went through everything, but she could not find it.

She heard Joan's feet hit the floor, and she tiptoed quietly to the door.

Joan was just getting dressed. "You up already, Felicia?" she echoed. "I must have overslept."

Then she saw the consternation in Felicia's face. She moved quietly over to her. "What is it, Felicia?" she asked in a coarse whisper.

"Have you seen my bookmark?"

Joan shook her head. "Not since you were showing it to the girls last night." She stiffened suddenly. "What's the matter, is it gone?"

"I must have misplaced it," her friend answered. "I can't find it anywhere."

Joan's forehead wrinkled. "You took it out of your Bible and passed it around so the girls could see it," she said. "And then I thought you put it back in your Bible. I can almost see you doing that."

Felicia turned back to her open suitcase and started to look for the bookmark once more.

"You–you don't suppose someone stole it, do you?" Joan asked at last, her voice weak and trembling. "It is beautiful – just the sort of thing that might attract a girl who has started picking up things that don't belong to her."

"I've got to get it back," Felicia said anxiously. "There isn't anything I own that means as much to me as that bookmark does. I–I just can't lose it!"

She finished looking through her suitcase. "It's made of silver and gold thread and has some rubies on it," she murmured, as though to herself, "but it isn't as valuable as a person would think. It's worth more to me than it is to anyone else."

Joan moved the nightstand and looked under the bed once more. "It just isn't here, Felicia," she said at last. "There's no use in looking for it any longer. You either lost it somewhere else or–"

"But I haven't been anywhere else!" she protested.

Joan's eyes narrowed. "Then it was stolen!"

Felicia's shoulders sagged, and for an instant, she swayed uncertainly. "Don't say anything about it to the girls yet," she said. "I want to be sure it's missing before I tell them."

"I suppose it might have dropped behind something," the Bailey girl said. "If it were mine, I'd be sure that's what happened." She looked around the big, sparsely furnished room.

"But I sure don't know where it could be."

By that time, Cynthia Prescott was awake. "What's the matter, Miss Cartright?" she asked. "Have you lost something?"

"Have you seen my bookmark?" Felicia replied. "I can't seem to locate it this morning."

Cindy sat bolt upright in bed. "It wasn't stolen, was it?" she demanded.

Felicia tried to sound calm and not particularly worried.

"I can't seem to find it this morning," she repeated. "I thought perhaps it got knocked off the table or something."

"The last time I saw it," Cindy said, "was when Mary Jane Forbes was looking at it."

Mary Jane! Felicia straightened and looked across the room at the girl's tousled blonde head. She had been terribly interested in the bookmark. Twice Felicia had surprised her looking at the bookmark. And even last night, when she had already looked at it twice before, she spent more time studying it than any of the other girls.

Felicia's heart seemed to become cold as ice.

Cynthia got up and dressed quickly. "I'll help you look for it."

"Thank you," Felicia answered. "I'm sure it's around here somewhere if we could just locate it."

The other girls awakened soon and, one by one, they joined the search until they had completely investigated every square inch of the big double cabin.

"It's been stolen," Winnie announced in her loud voice. "That's what's happened. We haven't found it, and we're not going to."

She turned to face Mary Jane before continuing.

"Somebody stole it. That's what happened."

"We don't want to be too hasty in saying that," Felicia countered gently. "We wouldn't want to accuse anyone without knowing for sure that the bookmark had been stolen and knowing the one who stole it."

Winnie's mouth twitched, but she said no more.

Although Felicia had been reluctant to believe that the bookmark had been stolen, she went to Mrs.

Markington after breakfast and told her everything that had happened. The camp director got to her feet and picked up a light jacket.

"I've been thinking that I ought to come down and talk with the girls," she said.

When they reached the Oriole and Raven Cabin, the girls were all still looking for Felicia's bookmark.

"But it's not here," Cindy said, acting as spokesman for the others. "We've been over this cabin a dozen times."

Mrs. Markington asked them to sit down on the floor and waited until they were all quiet. "I dislike coming to our campers like this," she began. "I would much rather trust each of you, believing that none of you would take anything that doesn't belong to you."

In the brief silence, she looked around coldly. "But apparently there is someone in the Oriole or Raven cabin who cannot do that. She feels that she has to have things that don't belong to her."

Winifred Stromer looked significantly in Mary Jane Forbes' direction. Felicia caught it plainly.

"When Miss Cartright and Miss Bailey came to me a short time ago and told me that several items had been stolen from your cabin, I suggested that we wait, thinking the matter might clear up by itself," the camp director said. "By that, I meant that there was a chance that the person who stole the cash, candy bars, and goggles would accept Christ as her personal Savior and confess what she had done.

That sort of thing has happened here on a number of different occasions in regard to other matters of discipline and personal problems."

She took a deep breath. "Now something much more serious than those items has been taken," she said. "Miss Cartright's antique bookmark has been stolen."

One of the girls started to cry quietly, wiping at her eyes with a tissue.

"You all know what it means to her and how badly she wants to get it back."

They nodded gravely.

"I am sorry to inform you girls," Mrs. Markington concluded, "that you will not be permitted to make your canoe trip until the bookmark has been found and returned to Miss Cartright."

Winnie caught her breath sharply. Mary Jane raised her eyes to Felicia's, a helpless, bewildered look glinting there.

Once Mrs. Markington dismissed them, the girls began to talk quietly in little groups. Mary Jane laid her purse on a bed nearby and came over to where Felicia was standing.

"M-M-Miss Cartright," she said, stammering.

Felicia turned to her. "Yes, Mary Jane."

"I–I–" her voice trembled. It seemed to Felicia that it trembled more than it normally did. "Miss Cartright, I–I'm awfully sorry your b-b-bookmark is missing. It was so beautiful."

Felicia smiled down at her. "Thank you, Mary Jane," she said. "Would you pray with me that it will be found? It does mean a great deal to me, and of course, I wouldn't want to see you girls miss out on your canoe trip."

The girl stood there for a short interval as though undecided whether she had something more to say or not. But at last, she turned and went slowly back to where her purse was lying. She acted so strangely that Felicia could not help watching her.

Mary Jane picked up her purse deliberately, looked around briefly, and took a step or two toward the door. As she did so, she opened her purse and took out a notebook. Something fell to the floor!

Felicia saw it even before anyone spoke.

"Your bookmark!" Cindy Prescott exclaimed incredulously. "Miss Cartright! There's your bookmark!"

CHAPTER 7

CAN MARY JANE BE TRUSTED?

For the space of a minute or two, they stared numbly at the bookmark on the floor. Silence hung like a cloud over them. Felicia's lips parted, but the words did not come.

Her heart breaking within her, she went over and picked up the bookmark. It lay like lead between her fingers.

Mary Jane blazed scarlet, her neck, her face, her forehead to the very roots of her hair. She looked up at Felicia, eyes wide and desperate with fear. "I–I didn't take your bookmark," she tremored, her agony betrayed in her voice. "It wasn't in my purse this morning, and I–I didn't take it!"

Felicia tore her gaze away from her forcibly and looked down at the bookmark she was turning slowly in her hand. There wasn't any joy in getting it back – at least not in the way she had gotten it back.

And in front of everyone too! If only it could have happened in private where only she and Mary Jane knew about it!

Winifred, who had been standing nearby, snorted derisively. "You can tell that to the others," she exclaimed, "but you'll never make me believe it! I know you stole the bookmark, my money, and Cindy's goggles too!"

Mrs. Markington came forward quickly and took Winnie by the arm. "I want all of you to go outside now," she said firmly. "This is a matter that we will handle."

"But Mary Jane stole my money," Winnie protested.

"We don't know that Mary Jane has stolen anything at all," the camp director retorted crisply. "Now run along to your next period – all of you."

"Come on, girls," Joan said, starting for the door. "Let's all go outside."

"But I don't see–" Winnie was grumbling as she left the cabin and passed from hearing.

Not until they were gone did Mrs. Markington and Felicia turn back to Mary Jane. The frightened girl could not bring herself to look up at them.

"Won't you sit down, Mary Jane?" Mrs. Markington said, her voice kind but firm enough to reveal that she would not tolerate any insubordination on the part of anyone.

The girl did as she was told, stiffly sitting on the edge of the chair. The tears began to steal out from beneath her eyelids one after another and trace their way down her cheeks.

"Why don't you tell us all about it?" Mrs. Markington said. "Start at the very beginning."

Mary Jane's eyes pleaded desperately with Felicia's. "There isn't anything to tell!" she blurted. "I–I know it sounds crazy, but I don't know how Miss Cartright's bookmark got in my purse. When I took out my notebook, it–it fell out on the floor. That–that's all I know about it, and that's the truth!"

Mrs. Markington frowned, and the fire returned to her voice, just a trace of it. "We want to help you, Mary Jane," she said sternly, "but we are not going to be taken in by a story that isn't true. We won't do a thing for you if you insist upon lying to us."

"I tell you I'm not lying!" she protested, her voice growing louder. "I'm telling you the truth. I didn't even know the bookmark was in my purse until it fell on the floor. Why, I even helped the other girls to hunt for it!"

She paused and turned to Felicia. "You've just got to believe me, Miss Cartright! You've got to!"

They questioned Mary Jane at length, but her story was not to be shaken. At last Mrs. Markington got to her feet. "You wait here for us, Mary Jane," she said, her voice softening. "Miss Cartright and I want to talk for a few minutes in private."

Felicia followed the camp director outside the

cabin to a place far enough away so they could not be overheard.

"I don't like to be thought of as an easy mark for a story," Mrs. Markington said, "but I can't help believing that girl. There's the ring of truth in what she tells us. I'm convinced of it."

A smile broke through to Felicia's lips. "I'm so glad to hear you say that, Mrs. Markington," she said. "I've felt that way about Mary Jane all along. I didn't see how she could be lying to us."

"We could both be wrong," Mrs. Markington said, "but I don't think so." She took off her watch and held it absent-mindedly.

"I suppose you realize that we have a big problem in this matter yet," she said. "All the girls in both cabins know about this. We believe that Mary Jane is not guilty; but if I know girls, they won't. I'm afraid they'll all be ready to think the worst about her."

Felicia nodded.

"And," Mrs. Markington said, "we still have the problem of learning who in your cabin or Joan's is the thief. Someone took that bookmark, and when the going got rough this morning and she became afraid that she was going to be found out, she slipped it into Mary Jane's purse."

They went back into the cabin and told Mary Jane that they both believed her story.

Her eyes found theirs, and she started to speak,

but she burst into tears. Felicia put her arm around the sobbing girl and comforted her as best she could.

At noon, they called the Orioles and Ravens together, with the exception of Mary Jane, who went for a walk with Joan, and Mrs. Markington talked with them.

"I want you to know," she said, "that Miss Cartright and I went into the matter thoroughly, and we have come to the conclusion that Mary Jane did not steal the bookmark or any of the other things that have been taken from your cabins."

The girls made no comment, but disbelief stood full in their eyes.

"I know why they said that," Cindy Prescott whispered to one of the girls as they filed out a few minutes later. "Mary Jane is Miss Cartright's pet. That's why. She wouldn't believe that she could possibly do anything wrong."

Felicia heard her but chose to ignore the remark.

During the next day or two, the girls showed Mary Jane in a hundred little ways that, regardless of whether Mrs. Markington, Felicia, and Joan thought she was innocent, they *knew* that she wasn't. They made a big fuss about locking up their personal things.

"You'd better hide your new notebook," Winnie Stromer said. "You know what happens to things around here if you don't."

Mary Jane felt their eyes on her and colored deeply.

The girls passed their canoeing, camping, and

first-aid requirements without difficulty and were ready to tackle swimming. Joan Bailey, who was the camp swimming director, was responsible for seeing that they passed the rigid requirements.

"I'm going to level with you," she told them frankly. "You may have thought the other requirements have been difficult, but there have been a few cases in which we have stretched a point or two when one of you almost passed, but still lacked a little. We aren't doing that with swimming. It is too important as far as this trip is concerned."

She put her hands on her hips. "I could pass you on part of this test in a group, but I don't think that's wise. We're going to take it individually, and we are going to insist that you pass each part of the test. If you don't, we are going to have to leave you here at camp."

The first two who tried failed by ten yards or so to pass their hundred-yard swim in deep water.

"Does–does that mean we won't get to go along?" they asked tearfully.

"Go ahead and pass the rest of the test," Joan told them. "If you pass all the other requirements, we'll give you one more opportunity to make the hundred-yard distance."

She raised her voice. "Who's next?"

Her gaze chanced upon Winifred Stromer who was standing to one side with Cindy Prescott and another girl. "How about you, Winnie?" she asked.

Winnie's face paled, and the corners of her mouth twitched uncertainly. "I–I'd just as soon wait until tomorrow, Miss Bailey, she said, "if it's all right with you. I–I've got sort of a headache."

Joan nodded. "We have plenty of others who would like to get it out of the way today. Mary Jane, how about you? Would you like to try now?"

The Forbes girl moved forward mechanically, her sallow face a pale, tightly drawn mask. Her lips moved wordlessly, but she did not speak.

Nevertheless, she moved out to the end of the pier and without any hesitation dived in. Her dive was razor sharp. She entered the water cleanly with only a trace of a splash and, when she came up, she swam with long, distance-eating strokes. At the fifty-yard marker, she reversed her direction and returned.

"I wish all of you girls could swim as well as Mary Jane does," Joan told them when she passed the last portion of her test. "That was excellent."

The other girls looked at Mary Jane stonily.

When the swimming period was over for the day, Felicia and Joan walked back to their cabin together.

"Well," Joan Bailey said, "tomorrow should see the last of our swimming tests. I think the girls have done very well, don't you?"

Felicia nodded. "I was surprised though. You announced that you weren't going to stretch anything to permit them to pass. The next thing, you tell two girls they can have another go at making their hundred-yard swim."

Joan laughed. "I know that. It so happens that those two girls were so afraid they weren't going to pass that they had been out in the lake practicing like crazy until we called on them. They were all worn out before they started. I don't think there's any question but that they can both pass their hundred-yard distance swim without trouble tomorrow when they're fresh."

"I was so glad that Mary Jane passed," Felicia said.

They neared the cabin. "It would have been bad if she hadn't." Joan paused. "Have you noticed how well she does almost everything she tries and yet she seems to have a feeling of inferiority?"

The following morning, the girls went down to the lake once more so that those who hadn't finished their swimming tests would have an opportunity to do so.

Winnie still hadn't reached the lake when Joan said to those who wanted to pass their tests to step forward. "Winnie!" she called. "We're waiting for you."

"I'll be right there!" She started to run, but only ran a few paces when she stepped in a hole and went sprawling. For a moment or two she did not get up.

Felicia saw her roll over and grasp her ankle with both hands. "Joan," she said softly, "I think she's hurt."

They hurried over to her.

"What's the matter, Winnie?" the Cartright girl asked, kneeling beside her.

"My ankle," she groaned. "I think I must have sprained it or something."

"That's too bad. Those things can be painful."

She reached out her hand and touched the girl's ankle tenderly. "It doesn't seem to be swollen."

"But it hurts!" She grimaced. "Oh, it hurts!"

By this time the other girls were crowding around her.

"Now I won't be able to pass my swimming test," Winnie moaned.

CHAPTER 8

IS WINNIE'S ANKLE SPRAINED?

Joan examined Winifred Stromer's ankle carefully. "Does it really hurt that much, Winnie?" she asked.

Winnie groaned. "Of course, it hurts! It hurts awful!" She reached down and touched her injured ankle with her fingers gingerly. "I can't stand the slightest pressure on it," she said.

"It doesn't seem to be swollen," Joan persisted. "At least not very much."

"I'm sorry it isn't hurt badly enough to suit you, Miss Bailey," she snapped irritably. "But it sure hurts badly enough to suit me."

The girls snickered.

"I didn't mean to make fun of you," Joan told her. "It's just that I've seen a number of sprained ankles, and all the others I've seen swelled very quickly, and some of them started to turn black."

She turned to a couple of Winnie's closest friends.

"Would you girls help her back to the cabin? We'll have the nurse come and take a look at it as soon as she comes out to camp."

Winnie looked up at Joan appealingly. "I–I suppose this means I won't get to go on the canoe trip," she ventured.

"We aren't going to worry about that now. The important thing is for you to get this ankle fixed up so you can enjoy the rest of your stay here."

Winnie's lower lip quivered. "Does–does that mean I won't get to go on the canoe trip?" she asked. Tears were not far away.

"We'll have to see about that when Miss Extrand has examined you."

When the nurse arrived, she looked the ankle over carefully. "It does seem to be a little larger than the other," Miss Extrand said, "but I'm like Miss Bailey. It seems strange that it would hurt so much. Have you ever had this ankle broken before?"

Winnie started. "Why do you ask?"

"Sometimes an ankle that has been broken will swell this way if it is used a great deal."

"N-No," she retorted quickly. "I've never broken my ankle, but I–I've sprained it a few times. It never does swell up much, but o-o-oh how it hurts!"

The nurse got out an elastic bandage. "I don't think it's a bad sprain. It'll probably be all right in a day or two."

She wrapped the ankle expertly, gave Winnie a pain pill, and left. "One of you had better take a look at it in the morning," she said. "And if it looks any worse or still hurts as it does, I think it would be wise to get her into a doctor. She may have a small bone chipped. That's the only thing I can think of that would hurt so much."

When Felicia went back into the cabin, Winnie's young face was twisted with pain, and tears filled her dark eyes. "Now I'm not going to get to go along on the canoe trip," she moaned. "That trip was the reason I talked Dad into letting me come to Camp in the Pines for the summer."

She swallowed hard. "Now I'm not going to make it."

"What makes you so sure about that?" Felicia asked.

"You heard Miss Bailey," Winnie went on. "She–she said that no one could go unless she had passed the swimming test. And I–I haven't passed it yet, and now I won't get a chance to."

"I'll talk with her tonight," the Cartright girl promised, "and see if it's possible for us to work something out."

Winnie brightened noticeably. "Would you?" she asked as though it were too good to be true. "Would you?"

The youthful counselor nodded and smiled.

The next morning, Joan and Felicia went in to see Winnie together. She was sitting up in bed.

"Hi," Joan said. "And how are you this morning?"

"All right, I guess." The pout had come back to her voice.

"How does the ankle feel today?"

"A little better," Winnie answered, "but not well enough to pass my swimming test – if that's what you mean."

"I wouldn't think of letting you go in the water now," Joan said. She started to unwrap the injured ankle.

"I have a Red Cross junior lifesaving certificate," the dark-haired girl said. "Would that show you that I can swim well enough so I could go along on the canoe trip?"

Joan pulled up a chair and sat down beside her.

"Of course, it would," she said. "Do you have your certificate with you?"

She shook her head. "No, but you could call my mother and–and talk with her about it if you want to. I've got the certificate in a frame hanging right over my bed."

Joan thought for a time. "I'll talk with Mrs. Markington," she said, "and see what she has to say. Perhaps we can work something out after all – that is, if Miss Extrand okays your going on a trip.

Winnie beamed. "Oh, it'll be all right by then!" she exclaimed happily. "I know it will!"

She raised up on one elbow. "Thank you, Miss Bailey. Thank you!"

Mrs. Markington thought it best to call Mrs.

Stromer and find out about the certificate for sure before giving Winnie permission to go along on the canoe trip.

"We must take every precaution to see that our girls are in a position to take care of themselves," she said, "in case trouble arises. We certainly don't want to have a serious accident of any kind."

She called Winnie's mother, but she did not answer.

She tried again in twenty minutes, in an hour, and two hours and a half, but the answer was still the same. Mrs. Markington sought out Joan and told her the result.

"The Stromers are not answering. I called both the home and office numbers. At the office, the receptionist said that Mr. Stromer was on vacation and could not be reached for a few days."

"Now that is too bad," Joan replied.

Winnie, who had hobbled to the dining room on crutches, listened stoically when Joan told her what Mrs. Markington had said.

"That's just my luck. I never get to have any fun." She took a deep breath and expelled it slowly. "Cindy Prescott and Donna Cramer both know how well I can swim. We swim together back home all the time. But I don't suppose that would make any difference. I don't suppose you'd take our word for it."

"That's right about Winnie's swimming," Cindy Prescott said. "We passed our junior lifesaving together last year."

"Winnie's a very good swimmer," Donna put in. "Why, I was with her last summer when she swam all the way across the lake. She swam a lot farther than either Cindy or me. I think she could pass her senior lifesaving right now, if–if it weren't for her hurt ankle."

Joan relayed the information to Mrs. Markington.

"Ordinarily," the camp director said, "I would be inclined to say that we would have to stick with the rules; but if the girl can actually swim as well as they say she can, it certainly wouldn't be fair to make her stay at home just because she hurt her ankle and can't pass our requirements."

Joan once more went back to Winnie. "Mrs. Markington thinks it's all right for you to go," she said.

"Oh, Miss Bailey!" she cried in a voice that carried through the dining hall, "that's just absolutely, positively wonderful."

"I'm glad you can go along," Joan told her. "I know how I'd hate to miss something as much fun as the canoe trip just because of a twisted ankle."

Later that evening, after the girls were in bed and asleep, Joan talked with Felicia about it as they went down to the kitchen to have a snack with the rest of the staff.

"I am glad that Winnie can go along," she confided, "but for some reason I feel uneasy about that story of hers."

"What do you mean?"

Joan sighed. "I don't know," she said. "I probably don't mean anything at all. I can't put my finger on it anyway. But the story seems too pat to me. It all fits together too well."

"You mean you're afraid she doesn't have her junior lifesaving certificate?" Felicia asked.

Joan paused, listening to the thin rattle of the wind in the leaves above them. "She must have it, or she wouldn't have been so willing to let us call her mother. Mrs. Markington did call her, you know."

They went into the kitchen where the other counselors were eating ice cream and cake and, for the moment at least, forgot all about Winnie Stromer, Mary Jane, and the items that had been stolen in their cabins. Indeed, as they went back to bed almost an hour later, it almost seemed as though none of those things had actually happened at all. They were just an ugly dream.

They were approaching the cabin in silence when they heard a furtive, stealthy sound in the Oriole side of the big double cabin.

Felicia stopped suddenly. "Joan!" she whispered, her voice hoarse, "what's that?"

"Somebody's out of bed. It looks as though you have a little disciplining to do."

"Look! Whoever it is has one of those small pencil lights!" Felicia managed. "You can see it through the window."

Joan grasped her arm. "Do you suppose it's the thief at work?"

In answer, Felicia moved forward. Joan was right beside her.

It was then that Felicia caught her foot on a tree root that protruded above the ground. She caught it at a time when she was already off balance and went sprawling noisily against the side of the cabin.

"Felicia!" Joan cried, "are you all right? Did you hurt yourself?"

The young counselor picked herself off the wall of the cabin and straightened slowly. "I–I guess so," she stammered.

"I don't suppose there's any use in saying anything to the girls about this," Joan went on. "There's no chance to catch whoever that was now."

"I don't know why I had to do a fool trick like that," Felicia said. "Here we were within a few feet of finding out who has been giving us all the trouble and I had to go and spoil it."

Joan laughed in spite of herself.

"What's so funny?" her friend wanted to know.

"I was just thinking that when anything like this usually happens, I'm the one who louses everything up. I'm glad to have it be you for a change."

They went on inside. The girls were lying there awake.

"M-M-Miss Cartright," one of them stammered uncertainly, "I-I-Is that you?"

"Who else were you expecting?" Felicia asked. "You girls should be asleep."

There was a brief, quiet interval.

"M-Miss Cartright?" the voice asked again.

"Yes, Donna?"

"I heard an awful noise just outside the cabin a little while ago. B-B-Bears don't try to come into these c-c-cabins, do they?"

Felicia laughed. "You forget about awful noises and bears and get to sleep."

She looked around as carefully as she could without arousing the suspicion of the girls, but nothing had been taken. Actually, there was no evidence that anyone had been up at all. Still, there was no doubting that she and Joan had heard someone moving around the cabin and had seen the pencil-thin beam of light. She went to bed, but questions crowded unanswered into her mind until she found it difficult to get to sleep.

On Monday morning after breakfast, the girls loaded their gear noisily into their canoes and got ready to leave. Earlier Miss Extrand had given Winnie permission to go along.

"Your ankle looks as though it's as good as ever," she said, "and I don't think it will give you any trouble, but you probably had better take it easy for a day or two, just to be sure."

"It'll be all right," Winnie said. "I know it will." Joan looked at her curiously but said nothing.

The rest of the girls at camp came out to see them off, enviously.

"I sure wish I could go along," a younger girl said.

Mary Jane, who was about to get into the canoe she was sharing with Donna Cramer, turned back to her. "You will," she answered. "When you come back next year, you ought to be old enough."

The trip began uneventfully enough. Joan, her detailed map close at hand, swung into the lead and guided them to the small river at the far end of the lake. From there they crossed a pond and had a short portage.

Felicia had chosen to paddle with Winnie Stromer that day. Winnie handled her paddle clumsily at first, but by noon she was using it like an expert.

Joan and Felicia stopped early the first afternoon at the far side of their first portage and supervised the girls putting up the tents. Once camp was ready and wood for the fire gathered, everyone went for a swim. Everyone, that is, except Winifred Stromer. She sat on a rock overlooking the water and watched.

"Aren't you coming in?" Joan called to her.

She shook her head. "I don't think so. My ankle hurts just a little tonight."

"The water would be good for it."

"No, thanks. I don't think I'll go in."

Both Felicia and Joan noticed her reluctance. "I don't get it," the Bailey girl said guardedly. "She insisted on carrying her share of the gear across the portage and didn't limp a bit. And she kept up with the rest of us. Now that we're swimming, her ankle suddenly hurts too badly for her to get in the water."

"I'm like you," Felicia answered. "I'm beginning to wonder if she can swim as well as she and her girlfriends have made us think that she can."

CHAPTER 9

ANOTHER THEFT

During the next two or three days, it seemed to Felicia and Joan that Mary Jane was at last beginning to come out of her shell.

"Nothing could have been better for her than this trip," Felicia said. "She is so able when it comes to handling a canoe, swimming, and all the rest of it. The other girls just can't help admiring her."

"I've noticed that some of them have been getting her to show them a little more about canoe handling or building fires with few matches and that sort of thing," Joan replied. "She should be building confidence in herself, and that's certainly what she needs."

"The thing I've appreciated most is her devotion to Jesus and the way she can quote Scripture. I've never heard anything like it!"

The canoe trip was fun for everyone, but it was more than that. It seemed to weld the girls closer together than they had ever been before. The thefts that had taken place seemed very far behind, almost as though they had never happened. And at night, when they had a time of Bible study and devotions around the campfire, it seemed that they were all drawn very close to God.

The first night out, one girl came to Felicia tearfully and accepted Christ as her Savior.

"I–I always thought I was a Christian," she said, "but since I've been to camp and especially since we've been out on this trip, I see that I'm not, and I–I want to be. I want to be saved."

Quietly, Felicia went over the plan of salvation with her, step by step, and finally knelt with her to pray with her. For a long while afterward, they sat beside the dying embers of the fire and talked. The moon passed behind a little cloud, and it grew very dark, but neither noticed. Joan and the other girls had long since gone to sleep.

"Now," the counselor said at last, "I think it would be good if you could find one of the other girls who has been a Christian for some time, who would meet with you every day for fellowship and prayer together."

Ellie Lombard nodded. "I think I'd like that."

"Is there any girl you would prefer?" Felicia asked.

"What about Mary Jane? She seems to know the Bible so well, and she lives what she believes." The new Christian paused. "Do you think she'd meet with me?"

Felicia's heart sang. "I'm sure she would. We'll talk with her the first thing in the morning."

The following night, Felicia asked for testimonies, and Ellie gave hers. It was halting and low, but nonetheless radiant.

"I–I think it was Mary Jane's testimony as well as the Bible lessons that–that made me see that my life wasn't all right and that I needed to trust Christ as my Savior. Her testimony and those Bible verses she has quoted have been going right through me."

Winifred Stromer, who was sitting on the log beside Felicia, stiffened noticeably, and a scowl darkened her young face. She was strangely quiet for the rest of the evening.

When the campfire service was over, Felicia turned to her. "Winnie," she said, keeping her voice down so the other girls could not hear, "tell me, are you a Christian?"

The girl beside her bristled. "Of course, I am."

"I don't want to doubt," Felicia went on, "but so often, especially among those of us who have been raised in a Christian home, we get to thinking we are saved when we actually haven't been. We're depending on our good works or on the fact that we go to a good church where the gospel is preached or perhaps even in the faith of our parents. Ellie was like that, but last night she realized that she had never confessed her sin and put her trust in Jesus Christ for salvation. She saw that she was lost."

Winifred stepped back a pace or two. Her face was sallow and taut with emotion, but her voice was bold and defiant.

"You can save your preaching for someone else, Miss Cartright," she said. "I already am a Christian."

She was breathing rapidly. "But if Mary Jane Forbes is a good example of what a Christian should be, I'm sure not proud that I'm a Christian. I might not be able to quote Scripture the way she does, but I'm not a thief."

Before Felicia could reply, she turned and went hurrying to her tent.

For a minute or two, the young counselor stood motionless, undecided whether to follow Winnie and talk with her about what she had said or not. Then she pivoted and went back to the tent she shared with Joan.

The following morning, Felicia and Joan were up before the girls as usual and went out on a little point not far from camp to read their Bibles and pray together. When they went back half an hour or more later, Joan saw that her duffel bag was on the ground. She went over to it and picked it up.

"I wonder how this got down," she murmured to herself. She took her wallet from the bag and opened it. "Felicia!" she exclaimed, her voice shrill with excitement. "It's happened again!"

The Cartright girl gasped.

"I'm missing thirty dollars," Joan said.

"Oh, no!" Felicia retorted miserably. "And just when I thought all of that business was over and done with."

"I don't know why I brought any money along," Joan continued. "I meant to leave it back at camp. In fact, I started off without my wallet, but I remembered that I'd need my fishing license; so I went back and got it."

The only sound was the gentle splashing of the waves against the rocks.

"This might prove to be a good thing after all," Joan said. "After your bookmark was stolen, I wrote down the serial numbers of my bills in my notebook. I figured that would give Mrs. Markington something to work on in case there was more trouble."

That day everything seemed to go wrong. They had a long, difficult portage that left the girls tired and irritable. Two of the girls, carrying a canoe over their heads, were attacked by hornets. Somebody else dropped a backpack filled with food in the lake ruining the pancake flour, and Cindy Prescott broke her paddle.

"Now I couldn't do anything about the pancake flour," Joan told her, "and I couldn't do much about the hornets, but I did figure somebody might break a paddle. So you're not going to get out of your share of the work after all."

Cindy laughed. "And here I thought I would be getting a free ride," she said.

"Oh, no," Felicia put in. "Nobody gets a free ride around here."

Winnie Stromer's eyes darkened. "Nobody, that is, except Mary Jane," she retorted, her lips curling. "She didn't have money enough to come here in the first place. She wouldn't even be here if somebody hadn't paid her way."

Mary Jane flushed scarlet, and for an instant or two, her lips trembled. Felicia took Winnie aside.

"That wasn't very kind," she said, her voice stern. "Mary Jane can't help it that her father is ill and didn't have money enough to send her here for the summer. She had nothing more to do with it than you had with the fact that your father has plenty of money."

Winnie's gaze met Felicia's for a brief moment. Then, without a word, she stormed to her canoe.

Mary Jane looked at Joan pitifully. "I–I'm not going to stay around here anymore," she stammered. "I'm going back home just as soon as we get back to camp."

Joan sought for words to comfort her, but there were none.

CHAPTER 10

GOING FISHING

Felicia and Joan were going to talk with Mary Jane and Winnie separately, but there wasn't time that morning.

"Look at those clouds," Joan said. "We'd better get a move on, or we'll be caught in a storm without having camp set up."

Felicia nodded. "We can't camp here," she said. "There isn't a clearing large enough. We'll at least have to go across the lake."

"Or out to one of the islands," Joan added. "According to the map, there are a number of large islands on this lake."

Felicia blew her whistle and called the girls to attention. "It looks as though there is a storm coming up," she said, "so we will have to hurry to find a good camp site and get our tents pitched before it hits."

"That's right," Joan put in. "I don't like to get wet, so we want you to lay on those paddles."

Winnie glanced up at the clouds uneasily. "Do you think it's safe to cross now?" she asked. "Isn't that storm apt to hit us before we make it?"

"What's the matter?" Cindy said, a strange note of laughter in her voice. "Are you afraid you're going to have to swim?"

Winnie flushed delicately and made a face at her.

Felicia caught the exchange and pondered over it as they paddled across the water.

She and Joan had decided to make camp on the first island that offered a good, sheltered camp site. The girls kept a close watch on the clouds and bent eagerly over their paddles. The heavily loaded canoes went plowing through the water.

Joan Bailey weighed the clouds in silence. There was probably wind in them and a great deal of lightning and rain, but the water now was placid, almost mirror-like. Here and there a skittering flurry of ripples marred the surface, and across the way, a fish jumped to send little concentric waves spreading wider and wider.

The first island lacked a suitable camp site, but the second was larger; and they found a beautiful little harbor protected on three sides from the wind.

"How does this look to you, Felicia?" Joan asked, gliding up to her friend's canoe.

"It looks fine," she answered. There was a quick

glance up at the clouds. "That storm doesn't look a great deal closer yet, but I suppose we'd better stop. We certainly don't want to get caught out in it."

"That's what I figure."

They pulled in to shore, brought their canoes far up on the bank, turned them over, and got to work pitching camp.

Felicia directed the pitching of the tents, taking great care to see that each was properly ditched and the walls banked with dirt; and Joan took three or four girls into the woods behind their camp site to cut firewood.

In less than an hour, the camp was ready, and the girls gathered around Felicia and Joan.

"Everything's done," Donna announced. "Now what are we going to do?"

The counselors looked up at the sky. The clouds were blacker than they had been and had probably moved a short distance above the horizon, but that was all.

"I don't think it's going to storm until tonight," Felicia said. "Do you?"

Joan shook her head.

"How many want to go swimming?" Felicia asked them.

A few hands went up. "I'd like to hunt for rocks," someone said.

"And I'd like to go fishing," Joan Bailey put in, "if anyone will go with me."

Mary Jane eyed her shyly. "I would," she said shyly, "if–if you'd like to have me."

"I don't know of anyone I'd rather take along," Joan said, smiling.

It was decided that those who wanted to go swimming could do so with Felicia, those who wanted to look for rocks and attractive pieces of driftwood could do that along the shore near the camp, and Joan and Mary Jane would go fishing.

"You won't need to fix any meat for dinner tonight," the Bailey girl called over her shoulder. "Mary Jane and I will bring back fish enough for everybody."

"Don't stay out that long," someone said. "You might be gone for a day or two."

"And keep a close watch on those clouds," Felicia reminded them. "A storm like that can sneak up on you at any time."

Joan got the casting rods and a small tackle box of lures they had brought along, and they took one of the canoes, paddling around the long finger of land that formed one side of the harbor.

"If I were you, Mary Jane," Joan said after a time, "I wouldn't pay any attention at all to what Winnie said back at the portage."

The youthful camper tried to speak, but her lips tremored until it was difficult. "I try not to," she managed after a time, "but it's hard. It's awfully hard. I just don't think I can take it anymore. She's–she's been after me ever since camp started."

"I think that is because she is under conviction," Joan went on, "and your testimony bothers her."

Joan put her paddle aside and cast a surface lure close to a large pad. "I'm sure nothing would please Satan more than to have you go home because Winnie has ridiculed you a little."

A big bass boiled out of the water to smash her lure. Joan gave a little squeal of excitement, and conversation ceased while she played the powerful fish. When she brought him up to the canoe, Mary Jane was ready with the net. She used it expertly to lift the bass out of the water.

Joan's smile broadened. "And they laughed when we told them that we'd furnish the meat for dinner tonight. This is only the beginning. Just wait until we get five or six like this. They'll all wish they had gone fishing with us."

Now that she had caught a fish, Joan insisted that Mary Jane cast while she use the paddle.

"You go ahead," the girl protested. "I'd just as soon watch."

"Not on your life. You're going to catch some of these fish too."

Mary Jane had fished before. That was apparent by her technique in which she tossed her lure and retrieved it.

On her third cast, she caught a fish considerably larger than Joan's. The whopper surged out of the water in a violent leap and hung there, shaking his head desperately to loose the hook, before dropping back into the water.

She kept the line taut as he ran for the boat, bored downward with a powerful blast that screamed yards of line from the reel. Momentarily he stopped, gathering strength, and came roaring out of the water in a spectacular leap that brought a shriek from both Joan and Mary Jane.

How many times he jumped out of the water they did not know. After the first three or four leaps they lost count, so intent were they in keeping pressure on the big bass. Five minutes passed, and then ten, before the fish began to tire. Then strength seemed to ebb from his runs, and he quit jumping from the water.

"He's coming in now," Mary Jane said quietly. "You can get the net, Miss Bailey."

"You'd think I was the one who was catching the fish," Joan muttered as she slid the net under the big mossback. "I'm the one who was excited."

Mary Jane smiled weakly.

For a couple of minutes after putting the bass on the stringer, they sat there looking at one another.

"I'll try to stay, Miss Bailey," she said suddenly. "It's going to be hard, but if you and Miss Cartright want me to, I–I'll try to stay."

"Thank you, Mary Jane," Joan said, her voice tender. "I know Felicia will be happy about it too. As happy as I am." She cast until she got a fish.

"We've already decided that we're going to talk

to Winnie about what she said," the counselor went on, "so that sort of thing won't happen anymore."

"Don't do that!" Mary Jane protested. "Please don't say anything to her about it. Everything will be all right. I–I just don't want to cause any trouble."

They had caught half a dozen fish and were paddling back to camp when Mary Jane mentioned the bills that had been stolen. "I–I heard about you getting some money stolen," she said uncertainly.

Joan stopped paddling and turned to look at her. "What do you mean?"

Mary Jane's eyes widened. "Didn't you?"

"Yes, but how did you find out?"

The camper didn't answer her immediately. "I hope those serial numbers help to find the guilty person," she said instead. "I've been praying and praying that she would be caught before she gets in any deeper."

Joan's eyes narrowed. "Mary Jane," she said, her voice growing firm, "how did you find out about the money being stolen and about my having the serial numbers of it? Who told you those things?"

"Cindy was up and happened to hear you and Miss Cartright talking this morning," she explained. "She said that you had thirty dollars stolen, but you don't really care because you have the serial numbers of the bills; as soon as we get back, you're going to have Mrs. Markington search each one of us and look at the numbers on our bills so you can find out who took them from you."

Joan took a long while before speaking. "Who did she tell it to?" she asked, "aside from you?"

"Oh, to everybody," Mary Jane retorted. "I heard it from Ellie Lombard."

Joan groaned inwardly. Now that was ruined. Whoever had the bills would surely destroy them or at least hide them somewhere so they wouldn't be found. "I shouldn't have opened my mouth," she muttered.

After a time, she glanced up at the clouds and then down at her watch.

"I really think we ought to be going in now, Mary Jane," she said, trying hard to hide her own disappointment. "Those clouds are getting closer, and it looks as though it might be going to break loose. I'd like to get dinner over with before it starts to rain if we can."

When they reached camp, the girls crowded around the canoe, gasping at the size of the fish.

"You really meant it when you said that you were going to catch enough for dinner," someone said.

"I always mean what I say," Joan retorted, laughing.

They cleaned the fish and fried them for dinner. Still the storm clouds held off.

"I think we're even going to be able to have our devotions before the rain," Felicia said. She glanced over her shoulder to see the forked lightning that was ripping from cloud to cloud and, every now and then, to the ground in the distance.

"I was hoping maybe it would pass us by," she continued, "but it doesn't look as though it's going to." Felicia started for the tent to get her Bible.

"Get mine, will you?" Joan called to her.

"Where is it?"

"Never mind." The Bailey girl got to her feet and ran over to her. "I'll get it myself." She went to her duffel bag and took her Bible out. Then, on impulse, she got her notebook and looked at it.

"Felicia," she said, her voice growing tense. "Someone has been into my things again."

"How do you know?"

"The page where I wrote the serial numbers of the ten-dollar bills I had with me is gone. Someone found my notebook and tore the page out!"

CHAPTER 11

CAUGHT IN A TRAP

Felicia Cartright's gaze met Joan's briefly. "But how did anyone know about them?" she asked. "I didn't tell anyone, and I'm sure you didn't."

"I didn't know I was telling anyone," Joan Bailey replied, "but I'm afraid I did just the same. Mary Jane let it slip that Cindy had heard what I said and told all the girls."

Concern marked Felicia's face. "What are we going to do now, Joan?" she asked numbly.

Her friend shook her head.

"It doesn't seem as though we ever will find out who has been taking these things," Felicia continued. "We've been praying and praying but don't seem to be any closer to an answer than we were the day Winnie's five dollars was stolen."

There was a sharp clap of thunder, and Felicia and Joan both turned to stare up at the darkening storm clouds. The lightning was closer now, sharper and more vivid.

"I don't know why I had to open my big mouth and spill everything where I could be overheard," Joan said after a minute or two. "That serial number thing was such a good idea. And it would have worked too. I just know it would have worked. Whoever took that money would never have thought of the serial numbers – until I spilled it all."

She shrugged her shoulders. "Now we're no closer to finding the guilty party than we ever were."

Felicia pushed her hair from her eyes with a quick, nervous gesture. "You know, Joan," she said. "I keep going over and over the characteristics of each one of the girls. They aren't all Christians, and not all of the Christians have dedicated their lives to Christ; but I can't think of a single girl that I feel would be capable of stealing the way it has been done here."

"I feel the same way," Joan retorted, "but somebody's doing it, that's for sure."

They stood there, looking at one another questioningly.

"What are we going to do now?" the Bailey girl asked.

"We've talked with them about it so many times that I'm beginning to wonder if it does any good," Felicia answered, "but we might get them together and at least let them know that we are aware of what's happening."

Her pal nodded in agreement. "I suppose that's about all we can do," she replied.

Joan took the whistle that was suspended on a cord around her neck and held it between her thumb and forefinger. "I'll call the girls together."

Felicia, who had forgotten about her own Bible temporarily, turned to her own duffel bag. As she looked into the duffel bag, she realized that something was amiss. It was nothing on which she could put her finger. Everything was in the same general order as she had put them. Still, her pulse quickened, and moisture formed on her forehead.

She took out her Bible and opened it. "Joan!" she cried involuntarily.

"What is it?" her friend demanded, coming over to her. "Did they take something from you too?"

Felicia nodded. "My bookmark," she managed. "It's gone again!"

By this time, the girls had begun to gather. They saw by the dismay on the faces of their counselors that something was wrong.

"What's the matter?" someone asked, her young voice taut with apprehension.

Behind the little circle of girls, the lightning was seldom gone from the clouds and the wind was beginning to freshen. It was still light, but it would not be for long. The sun was below the clouds, and already the far shore was becoming blurred and indistinct.

Felicia and Joan looked from one girl to the other, uncertain of what to say or how to begin.

"What is the matter?" Cindy Prescott wanted to know.

Felicia breathed deeply, and her face grew stern. "I think all of you had better sit down for a few minutes," she said, choosing her words carefully. "There is a matter that Miss Bailey and I would like to go over with you again."

"It's going to storm," Cindy Prescott said. "We'd better check the canoes again."

"The canoes are all right just as they are," Joan told her. "I checked them myself a few minutes ago."

"What's been taken now?" Winifred Stromer asked under her breath.

Felicia turned to her. "Winnie," she said, "what made you say that?"

"I don't know," she blustered. "I guess it was because every time we get called together, you announce that somebody has taken something and you're going to get real, real mad if we don't come and confess to you."

She would have said more, but Felicia's icy stare choked the words in her throat, and she flushed uneasily.

"You were right about one thing, Winnie," the counselor continued, "something has been stolen. This time the thief took thirty dollars from Miss Bailey's wallet and my bookmark again."

Everyone turned instinctively toward Mary Jane,

whose cheeks went sallow. She stared at the ground almost guiltily.

"I know who did it," Winnie put in after a brief, uneasy silence, "but you probably won't believe me."

"If you have any proof," Felicia said, "we'll be glad to hear it privately. If you are just going to make an accusation, we'd rather you didn't."

Winnie Stromer's voice raised. "I might have known you'd want to hush it up, but I'm not going to. I'm going to tell what I know whether you want me to or not."

She turned toward Mary Jane. "I saw Mary Jane Forbes go into your tent this afternoon for something and then go to her own tent and put something in her backpack. If you look in there, you'll find what you're looking for!"

Mary Jane gasped aloud. "But I didn't," she protested. "I didn't go into your tent for anything, and I didn't put anything that belonged to you into my backpack."

"That's a serious charge, Winnie," Joan said. "A very serious charge."

"If you don't believe me, just go and look." By this time Winifred Stromer had gotten to her feet. "Your bookmark fell out of her purse once before, but neither you nor Mrs. Markington would believe that she took it. What do you think now?"

A harsh clap of thunder stunned them all to silence.

"You can look through my things," Mary Jane

said. "I want you to—I want you to see that I didn't take anything from you."

Mechanically, because she could think of nothing else to do, Felicia took Mary Jane's icy fingers and led the others over to the tent she shared with Ellie Lombard.

"I know Mary Jane didn't steal anything from anyone," Ellie said loyally. "She's a good Christian. She wouldn't do anything like that."

"Just wait," Winnie retorted. "Just you wait! You'll see whether I'm telling you the truth or not – unless she got scared and moved them to someplace else in the last couple of hours."

Felicia glanced quickly in Winnie's direction and started to speak, but Mary Jane was opening her bag, and Felicia moved closer, not wanting to look, but unable to turn away.

"It—it's too dark in there to see much," she said. "I'll get my flashlight."

The beam of light revealed the ten-dollar bills and the bookmark, carelessly poked beneath Mary Jane's hat.

"There!" Winnie exclaimed triumphantly. "There they both are! Now will you believe me when I tell you that Mary Jane is the thief? She's the one who stole my five dollars and Cindy Prescott's candy bars and goggles, and now these things. She's done it all!"

Mary Jane's face was taut and drawn. Her lips parted, but no words came out.

Winnie turned to Felicia. "I was right, wasn't I?"

"That depends," the counselor said evenly. "Just what did you see Mary Jane do?"

The young camper's eyes narrowed. "What do you mean?"

"I'd like to have you start at the beginning and tell us just exactly what you saw," Felicia said. "We want to know what you did and what Mary Jane did – every single thing that you can remember."

Winnie cleared her throat. "Well," she said, "I had been looking for rocks for quite a while and got tired; so I came up here to lie down for a few minutes when I saw someone in your tent."

"And you were close enough to see clearly who it was?"

"Oh, sure," Winnie retorted. "I'd know Mary Jane anywhere."

"Then what did she do?"

"She took something out of Miss Bailey's duffel bag, and then she went over to yours and had it open quite a long time."

"I didn't!" Mary Jane protested involuntarily. "I wasn't near your tent."

"Let Winnie tell her story," Felicia said.

"And then Mary Jane came to the door of the tent and looked out to see that no one had seen her," she continued. "Then she ducked out and went running over to her tent just as fast as she could."

"And she didn't see you when she looked out of our tent?" Joan asked.

"No," Winnie answered, "she didn't see me. I was back in the shadows, sort of."

"I see."

Felicia brushed the back of her hand over her forehead uneasily. "And after she went to her tent, what did she do?"

"I–I don't know for sure. She just went down to the beach, I guess."

Felicia took a step or two toward Winnie. "Winifred," she began, "when did all of this take place?"

"I don't know. What difference does that make?"

"It might not make any difference," Felicia said, "and it might make a lot of difference. What time did Mary Jane take the bookmark and money from our tent?"

The young camper squirmed. "I–I don't know for sure."

"But you said that it was after you had been looking for rocks a while, didn't you?"

Winnie nodded. "I suppose I'd been looking for rocks half an hour or maybe an hour when my ankle got to hurting, and I decided to go up to the tent and lie down."

Felicia's eyes snapped. "You're sure of that?"

"Positive!" Her voice rose indignantly. "You act as though I'm the one who's done something wrong instead of Mary Jane!"

"Have you forgotten where Mary Jane was this afternoon while the rest of you went swimming or looked for rocks?" Felicia asked. "Mary Jane is the only girl who couldn't possibly have had anything to do with it. She left with Joan in the canoe, and they were gone until just before dinner!"

Winnie Stromer's face went white. Her mouth sagged open, and wild, hysterical fear came to her eyes.

"M-m-maybe I was mistaken about the time," she stammered. "I must have been. It–it was probably earlier."

"But you said you had been looking for rocks," Felicia insisted. "You didn't look for rocks until after camp was set up. And as soon as that happened, Joan and Mary Jane went fishing; so she couldn't possibly have done what you said she did."

Winnie stared around the group in growing desperation. Tears coursed down her cheeks. She whirled and went running into the woods.

"I–I didn't want to say anything," one of the girls ventured timidly some moments later, "but I saw Winnie do just what she said Mary Jane had done, only I didn't think anything about it at the time. It wasn't until she started to accuse Mary Jane that I even remembered."

Mary Jane Forbes, shoulders trembling convulsively, started to sob.

CHAPTER 12

OUT IN THE DARKNESS

Felicia put her arm around Mary Jane's shoulder comfortingly, but she was not thinking of the quietly sobbing girl who stood beside her. She was thinking of Winnie Stromer who was alone somewhere out in the darkness.

"Joan," she said, her voice hushed with concern, "do you think we ought to go out and get Winnie and bring her back here now?"

"In a few minutes," the other counselor answered. "I think it would be better to let her get her crying out first."

The campers looked at one another and at their counselors uneasily.

"Miss Cartright," Cindy Prescott said, "is–is it all right if I move into a tent with a couple of the other girls?"

Felicia looked down at her. "Why?" she asked simply. "I thought Winnie was a good friend of yours."

"She–she was." Defiance leaped to the girl's eyes. Defiance and anger. "But I don't want to sleep in the same tent with a–a thief!"

"What are you going to do about her?" somebody else broke in. "Are you going to make her parents come and take her home?"

The young counselors looked at one another, but it was Felicia who turned to the girls and raised her voice above the rumble of the wind and the waves.

"There's something that we want to tell you all," she began, praying for guidance and the words to say that she felt in her heart, "and I think it's better to do it before Winnie comes back."

The girls had been murmuring to one another, but now they were silent.

"What Winnie has done is a terrible thing," Felicia continued. "I'm not trying to make it sound any less evil and wrong than it is. She not only stole those things herself, but she tried her best to blame it on Mary Jane, who is innocent."

There was lightning and thunder almost continually now, but the girls scarcely noticed it. They stood in silence, their faces upturned to Felicia, clinging to every word she spoke.

"It isn't going to help Winnie or us if we should turn our back on her now and have nothing whatever to do with her. And it isn't going to help her if we all start to talk about her. I hope none of you will say anything about what has happened tonight – either among yourselves or to Winnie. Let's join our hearts in prayer for her."

"But she took some things that belonged to me," Cindy Prescott protested, "and all the time she was pretending to be my best friend."

"What does the Bible say we should do when someone wrongs us?" Felicia asked her gently.

A bolt of lightning split the darkness, and thunder reverberated from shore to shore. One of the girls screamed involuntarily.

Felicia stopped short. "You'd better stay here with the girls, Joan," she said. "I'm going to get a flashlight and go out after Winnie."

Mary Jane looked up at her. "May I go along, Miss Cartright?" she asked.

Felicia started to refuse but checked herself. "Of course, Mary Jane. I'd love to have you."

She thought that Winnie had only gone to the edge of the clearing to a little hill overlooking the lake. There was a place there where two or three of the girls had gone late in the afternoon to be alone and read their Bibles and pray. Felicia and Mary Jane went up there first, picking their way up the stony path hand in hand.

"I feel so sorry for Winnie," Mary Jane said, her voice small and thin. "I know just how miserable she must feel."

"I'm sure she is miserable," the counselor replied. "Sin always makes us feel that way."

Winnie wasn't on the hill where Felicia thought she would be, nor was she back in the trees behind the tents. The counselor stopped and looked around in the darkness. Fear clawed at her throat with icy fingers, and a terrible weakness took hold of her.

"She's not around anywhere, Mary Jane," she managed. She tried to sound very confident that Winnie would be found soon, but her concern leaked through to edge her voice.

The girl's small hand began to tremble in hers. "Maybe she went down to the lake shore," she suggested. "I like to do that sometimes to watch the waves and listen to them slap against the rocks."

They turned and made their way across the corner of the clearing to the place where they had put the canoes for the night.

The wind, that had been freshening for the last hour or so, ceased suddenly, and a tense, expectant hush settled over the lake – a hush broken by the sound of waves against the rocks and, every now and then, by the deep-throated grumbling of thunder. A few drops of rain spattered down, and Felicia shivered apprehensively.

Near the canoes they stopped.

"I don't think she's around here either," Felicia said.

And then there was a brilliant flash of lightning that knifed downward and quivered in the air momentarily. For a brief instant, it lit the lake from island to shore. In that instant, they saw something etched vividly against the blackness – something that froze them both!

Mary Jane Forbes grasped Felicia's arm and squeezed it convulsively.

"M-M-Miss Cartright!" she gasped. "Did you see what I saw out there?"

Felicia glanced down at the canoes numbly and counted them – as though she could not believe what she had seen. But no! One of them was gone! A canoe was gone, and Winifred Stromer was out on the lake alone!

For a brief space of time, Felicia could not move. Her throat tightened convulsively, and her head spun. She squeezed Mary Jane's hand even more tightly. "Winnie!" she exclaimed under her breath. "No!"

"W-W-What are we going to do?" Mary Jane asked weakly.

The sound of her voice seemed to free Felicia from the grip of terror that held her. She whirled and ran a few paces toward camp, calling out as she ran.

"Come quick, Joan! Winnie's taken one of the canoes and is out on the lake!"

An instant or two later, Felicia and Mary Jane were surrounded by frightened, tense-faced campers.

"Where is she?" Joan demanded. "When did she go?"

"She's out there about a quarter of a mile," Felicia

exclaimed, trying to keep calm but failing miserably, "so she can't have been gone too long."

"We've got to get her!" Joan exclaimed. "That storm's going to hit full force any minute! And if it does, she can't handle a canoe well enough to keep from capsizing."

"And–and she can't swim!" Cindy Prescott cried miserably.

Joan stooped impulsively and grasped the girl by her shoulders. "What did you say?" she asked roughly.

"W-W-Winnie doesn't have her junior lifesaving certificate like–like I said she had," Cindy blurted. "She could only swim across our pool back home. And then she–she'd have to swim it at the shallow end so she could stop and rest if she got tired."

"But you told me she was a good swimmer!" Joan said. "You told Mrs. Markington and I that Winnie could swim as well as you!"

Cindy began to cry convulsively. "I know I lied to you, but Winnie wanted to go along on this canoe trip so bad, and she knew she'd never be able to pass her swimming test, so she talked Donna and me into lying for her."

"And she faked that sprained ankle!" Joan exclaimed. "I knew it! I had a hunch about that ankle!"

While they were talking, Felicia, Mary Jane, and one of the other girls turned a canoe over hurriedly and carried it down to the water's edge.

"You look after things here, Joan!" Felicia called to her. "I'm going after Winnie!"

"Let me go along, Miss Cartright!" Mary Jane pleaded.

"I can't let you, Mary Jane! It's going to be storming in a minute or two."

The wind raised suddenly to bring truth to her words, and it began to rain.

"But I can swim and handle a canoe, and you may have to have help out there!"

Felicia did not tell her she could or couldn't go but made no protest when Mary Jane stepped expertly into the lithe, fiberglass canoe and picked up her paddle.

The waves had not gone down during the brief lull in the wind, but now that the storm broke over the lake, they were quickly lashed to a foam-laced fury. Rain swept across the lake in a blinding torrent that drenched them to the skin in a single instant. Felicia shook her head doggedly and drove the paddle deep into the water. The canoe moved forward.

Mary Jane, in the rear, caught the rhythm of Felicia's stroke almost instinctively and helped to keep the canoe's slender nose knifing into the deep-troughed waves. They dug their paddles blade deep into the water and bent their backs to them, fighting against the full fury of the wind and rain. The canoe inched forward painfully. It came up sluggishly on the crest of one wave only to drop into the trough behind it. And now and again the wave following would slam in at a slight angle to send its crest curling over the gunwales.

Every stroke, every searing breath was a prayer as Felicia battled the storm. She was thankful for Mary Jane behind her. Alone, the task would have been all but impossible.

In the flashes of lightning, Felicia caught glimpses of Winifred. The other canoe was making little headway now. Indeed, she was only able to keep the nose headed into the waves part of the time. A heavy wave would slam into her frail craft, and it seemed as though she lost all control for a moment or two. The bow would swing dangerously to one side or the other, and for an agonizing period, the canoe would lay crossways of the waves. It would ride over the crest with a dangerous lurch and almost disappear from view as it plunged into the trough on the other side.

"Winnie!" Felicia shouted in desperation. "Don't give up! We're coming! Use your paddle!"

But the wind hurled the words back into her teeth.

Grimly, Felicia quickened the pace of her own paddling. Mary Jane caught the increased tempo and matched it with long, powerful strokes of her own. How they were able to accomplish it, neither of them knew. It seemed that they were putting forth every effort before. But now the canoe began to move even faster. It seemed to rise above the fury of the waves – to slam over one and knife into the next, shaking off the water in a foam-etched plume.

The minutes passed; and as they did so, the gap between the two canoes narrowed. They were three hundred yards away and then two hundred and fifty. Felicia measured it mentally in the flashing lightning.

If only Winnie could hold out! If only she could fight a little longer – until they had time to fight their way to her side.

What would she do then? For the first time that question gripped Felicia. Until now, she had been so concerned about reaching Winnie that she had not thought about what they would do when they did. For a brief instant, panic gripped her heart.

What would they do? What could they do?

A moment later, Winnie let the canoe turn sideways against the waves once more. It rolled wildly as a huge breaker slipped from under it, and she clutched the gunwales with both hands. It was then that she saw Felicia and Mary Jane for the first time. She stared at them disbelievingly as the canoe lurched over another big wave.

"Winnie!" Felicia cried out. Paddle! Paddle!"

The distance between them was less than fifty yards and, because Winnie's canoe was drifting helplessly with the waves, it was narrowing rapidly.

"Paddle!" Felicia almost screamed. "Paddle! Paddle!" She heard! Thank God she had heard!

Winnie Stromer did not move for one long, agonizing instant. The very sound of Felicia's voice drifting eerily to her through the wind and the rain seemed to have stolen what strength she had. The canoe rose sluggishly to the crest of a huge wave and skidded down to the trough behind it. Winnie chose that moment to release her grip and make a dive for the paddle. The canoe shipped water as she did so.

She screamed frantically, dropped the paddle, and grasped for the gunwales with both hands. Her sudden movement was too much for the sluggish, uncontrolled canoe. It lurched again violently and flipped over, throwing Winnie into the icy water.

Felicia cried out in desperation!

CHAPTER 13

LOVE CONQUERS

For a brief, agonizing interval, Winifred Stromer was not in sight. All Felicia and Mary Jane could see was the silver bottom of the canoe against the black of the water.

As though in wild defiance, the rain increased its fury, and the wind raged until it blew the tops off the waves and sent one breaker after another crashing into the prow of Felicia's canoe. Lightning streaked down among the trees ahead to the sharp crackle of thunder and tremored from cloud to cloud, lighting all the lake in a brief, blinding flash.

Something died within Felicia as she realized that Winnie had not come up. "Oh, God!" she prayed inwardly, throwing her full weight against the paddle. "Help us to get to her! Help us to get to her!"

Time seemed to grasp their canoe and hold them

motionless! Seconds became minutes and hours, and still Winnie Stromer was not in sight.

The overturned canoe disappeared behind a wave, and when it came up, Winnie was there beside it. Just her head showed above the water, and her arm looped over the prow of the capsized craft.

She was there! And for the moment at least, she was all right! A quick prayer of thanksgiving went up from Felicia's heart. By this time, the two canoes were a scant twelve feet apart.

"Hang on, Winnie!" Felicia cried out encouragingly. "We'll have you in a jiffy! Don't give up now!" Felicia and Mary Jane's canoe nosed the capsized craft.

"Get your end of the canoe close to her!" Felicia shouted to her companion. "We'll have to have her hang on so we can take her ashore. She can never get in here without upsetting us in this storm!"

But Mary Jane had already anticipated what she had in mind. Changing her stroke expertly, she brought the canoe around until she was within a foot or so of the girl in the water. "Winnie!" she cried. "Are you all right?"

Winifred Stromer said nothing.

"Winnie!" Mary Jane cried again. "Winnie, you've got to take hold of our canoe so we can tow you ashore! Turn around and reach out with your other hand!"

Still, she neither spoke nor moved!

"Hurry, Mary Jane!" Felicia ordered. "We can't hold them together much longer!"

"Winnie! Do you hear me?" When she got no response, she reached out in desperation and grasped Winnie's arm. "Let go, Winnie!" she shouted above the storm.

"Don't!" The terrified girl almost shrieked the word. "Don't!" She fought to free herself from Mary Jane, but the slender girl in the canoe clung to her tenaciously. With relentless pressure, she pried Winnie's arm free from the overturned canoe and pulled her, screaming in protest, to the other craft. Winnie was sobbing now, and her grip on the side of the canoe was feeble.

"I've got her, Miss Cartright!" Mary Jane exclaimed, "but I think I'd better hold on to her if–if you think you can manage the paddling alone. She's awfully weak."

"Going with the waves is a cinch," Felicia cried above the wind.

There was a song of thanksgiving and praise in her heart as she let the wind turn the prow of the canoe. As it started to come about, she shoved hard with her paddle to force it around before a wave had opportunity to crash into them broadside.

Although the intensity of the storm had not less-ened, as soon as they began to run with the waves, it seemed to have eased off appreciably. The sturdy little craft stopped its bucking and began to edge through the waves effortlessly. It rolled some and shipped a little water on the side where Mary Jane was holding

Winnie, but it seemed to be as nothing compared to the fight they had in going the other way.

Felicia paddled slowly with long, smooth, deliberate motions. "How is it going?" she called to Mary Jane after five minutes or so.

"Fine." She looked down at Winnie. "You're all right, aren't you?"

The frightened girl in the water nodded.

They were a hundred yards or so from shore when the powerful beam of Joan Bailey's electric lantern picked them up. The girls were all standing with her in the rain and wind. "Felicia!" Joan shouted. "Are you all right? Are you all right?"

"Fine!" Her voice rode to them on the wind. "We've got Winnie!" Moments later, they brought the runaway girl to shore.

"How is she?" Cindy Prescott asked tearfully. "Is she all right?"

Felicia had gotten out of the canoe and was on one side of Winnie. Joan was on the other side.

"Is she all right?" somebody else asked.

"She's all right," Joan said. "Now I think you had all better go back to your tents. We've got to get Winnie into some dry clothes."

"W-W-Why did you come and get me?" Winnie asked Felicia in a taut, strained voice. "Why didn't you just let me go?"

"You've had a terrible experience, my dear," Felicia

told her. "We won't talk about it now. You need to get into some dry clothes and get some rest."

Numbly, Winifred Stromer allowed them to lead her up to their tent.

Mary Jane, who had stayed beside them, touched Joan on the arm. "I'll make some hot chocolate if you think she'd like to have some."

Joan turned. "I know she would, but you can't build a fire in this storm."

"I'll fix a fire under one of the canoes," the young camper said. "Dad taught me how." She went hurrying away to gather birch bark and dry twigs that were still on the trees. Although water dripped from the wood, it had not had opportunity to soak in.

Propping one side of a canoe up with a short paddle, she fixed her birch bark and twigs and, in a few minutes, had a small fire burning briskly. She mixed powdered milk with water and condensed milk to add flavor and strength, and, in a short time, had a pot of steaming hot chocolate.

Winnie took it gratefully. Her eyes met Mary Jane's, and then she looked away.

The young Christian looked at her gently. "Is–is there anything I can do for you, Winnie?" she asked. "Is there something you'd like to have?"

Winnie's throat tightened. She tried to speak, but tears came again.

Felicia put her arm around the young camper's shoulder comfortingly.

"Why didn't you leave me out there?" she asked. "Why didn't you let me go?"

"Don't try to talk now, Winnie. You need some rest. There'll be plenty of time for talking in the morning."

The girl swallowed hard. "But I want to talk now," she blurted. "I want to talk!"

Mary Jane started to back away. "If there's nothing else you need me to help with," she said, "I think I'll go back to my tent."

"You'd better," Felicia told her gratefully, "and get some dry clothes on. We don't want you catching pneumonia."

She would have left, but Winnie grasped her hand. For a long minute, she held it in a tense, viselike grip. "M-M-Mary Jane," she stammered, "you came out and–and risked your life to help save me after the way I–I treated you."

Mary Jane flushed, and she tried to pull away. Her lips parted, but she said nothing.

"I've been meaner to you than I–I've been to anyone else in my whole life," Winifred continued brokenly. "After all that, you helped save my life and even worked in the cold making that hot chocolate for me. Why, I wouldn't even have done that for a–a friend, let alone someone who had treated me the way I've been treating you!"

"I think I can tell you why Mary Jane has been nice to you, Winnie," Felicia said gently. "It's because she's a Christian. Because she has trusted Christ as her Savior and is trying to live for Him."

The only sounds were those of the wind and the pounding rain.

"What are you going to do to me?" Winnie demanded suddenly, the fright coming back to her voice.

"What do you mean?" Felicia asked.

"For taking all those things and blaming it on Mary Jane." She took a deep breath.

"We'll have to tell Mrs. Markington all about it," Joan said. "She's the camp director and has a right to know, but I'm sure you'll find her very kind and understanding."

"Will—will I have to go home?" The words came out tearfully.

"She's going to want to be sure that you have learned your lesson," Felicia said, "and that it doesn't happen again."

"Oh, you won't have to worry about that!" Winnie said firmly. "I'll never take anything that doesn't belong to me again as long as I live."

She swallowed hard. "I was so afraid I was going to get caught that I–I felt terrible all the time, but I–" Her voice trailed off into silence.

The counselors and Mary Jane looked at her. "The other day I talked with you about Jesus, Winnie," Felicia said, "and you told me that you had already trusted Him as your Savior – that you are a Christian."

A strange, haunted look glinted in the girl's dark eyes.

"Are you?" Felicia asked.

"I just told you that so–" Her voice choked off, and she wet her lips with the tip of her tongue. "I just told you that so you wouldn't bother me anymore."

"Wouldn't you like to accept Christ as your Savior now?" Joan suggested. "Wouldn't you like to get straightened out with God?"

Tears came to Winnie's eyes once more. "God wouldn't want me," she said hesitantly. "Not after what I've done."

"That isn't what the Bible says," Felicia told her. "The Bible says that God will not reject those who come to Him."

"But I've done such terrible things. I even lied to you about being a good swimmer and about my ankle being hurt and–and about my parents being home when you called them. I knew they were on vacation. That's why I told you to call."

"We knew most of that," Felicia said, "and guessed the rest. But we didn't find out until tonight after you took the canoe and tried to run away."

Winnie's lower lip began to tremble once more. "God wouldn't want me," she repeated, and there was a desperate longing in her voice.

"He wanted the Apostle Paul," Joan said, "and Paul had been a murderer. He had been killing Christians.

Yet God appeared to him on the road to Damascus, and Paul became an outstanding Christian."

The hurt in Winnie's face deepened. "But I could never live a good Christian life," she protested. "I couldn't be like Mary Jane. I'm too weak! It's just no use. I couldn't be a Christian."

"None of us can live a Christian life in our own strength, Winnie," Felicia said. "The Bible tells us that. But God will help us to live the way He wants us to live. He'll give us the strength to do it."

Winnie looked up at Mary Jane. "Would–would you help me?" she asked, "the way you've been helping Ellie Lombard."

"Of course, I will," Mary Jane smiled tenderly.

In a few minutes, they all knelt together and Winifred Stromer accepted Christ as her personal Savior.

* * *

Mrs. Markington sat quietly in her office listening as Winnie blurted out her confession. Felicia and Joan sat on either side of the frightened girl.

"I–I've gone to the people I took things from," she said, "and g-g-gave back what I took or paid them for it if I couldn't give it back – like those two candy bars I stole. And I–I asked them to forgive me."

"I'm glad you've done that, Winnie," the camp

director said. "That helps to show that you really mean business with us and with the Lord."

"And whatever you do about sending me home is all right with me. I want to make things right – whatever it takes."

Mrs. Markington was a long while in answering. "I don't think this course of action will be necessary," she said at last. "You have made a stand for Christ and are showing that you are truly sorry for what you've done and want to make amends. We don't want to be vindictive."

She picked up a pencil and toyed with it for a moment or two thoughtfully. "On the other hand, we can't let something as serious as this pass by without some form of punishment. I'll talk with Miss Cartright and Miss Bailey, and we'll work out something – a denial of certain privileges for the rest of the camp period."

Relief flooded Winnie's taut face. "Oh, thank you!" she exclaimed gratefully. "Thank you!"

"And," Mrs. Markington continued, her voice growing stern once more, "we will have to put you on probation. If anything else like this happens, then we will have to call in the authorities and you will be dismissed from camp. If it doesn't, you will have nothing to be concerned about."

"You won't have to worry about that," Winnie told her. "I've learned my lesson. And besides, I'm a Christian now."

Mrs. Markington smiled once more.

As Felicia and Joan rose to go, they heard a familiar voice outside. "Hey girls, wait for me! Wait for me!"

Felicia beamed. "It looks as though Mary Jane learned her lesson about feeling inferior to the other girls too," she said.

Joan's throat choked and, for a moment or two, she could not speak. "Already," she said at last, "I think this has been the most glorious summer we've ever spent!"

THE
FELICIA CARTRIGHT
SERIES

Felicia Cartright, a petite blonde who is one of the most popular students at Wellington School for Girls, has a surprising inclination toward mysteries. If a mysterious situation arises, it either makes its way to Felicia, or Felicia somehow finds it. Though this is a bit trying for her happy-go-lucky roommate, Joan Bailey, it does prevent life from becoming monotonous. It also enables Bernard Palmer, the popular author of the "Danny Orlis" books, to write an entertaining series of stories for girls aged twelve to eighteen.

The mysteries range from a valuable missing antique to an attempt by claim jumpers to steal a deposit of tungsten ore. There's excitement and action galore—but there's also spiritual guidance and blessing because Felicia and her partner-in-adventure love the Lord and take Him into account in all their experiences.

AVAILABLE FROM WWW.ANEKOPRESS.COM